# A POLITICS OF LOVE

## A HANDBOOK FOR A NEW AMERICAN REVOLUTION

## MARIANNE WILLIAMSON

HarperOne

*An Imprint of HarperCollinsPublishers*

*For those who came before,*

*and those who will come after*

HarperCollins books may be purchased for educational, business, or sales promotional use. For information, please email the Special Markets Department at SPsales@harpercollins.com.

FIRST HARPERCOLLINS PAPERBACK EDITION PUBLISHED IN 2021

*Designed by Yvonne Chan*

Library of Congress Cataloging-in-Publication Data is available upon request.

ISBN 978-0-06-304181-3

21 22 23 24 25  LSC  10 9 8 7 6 5 4 3 2 1

# CONTENTS

# PREFACE

In January 2019, I announced I was a candidate for president of the United States.

For almost forty years I had watched with great sadness—commenting on it repeatedly in my books and lectures—as America slipped gradually from a functioning democracy into a functioning plutocracy. Whereas average middle-class American workers in the 1970s had a decent job with good benefits, owned a home and a car, and could send their kids to college and take a yearly vacation (and such families could usually survive on a single income), all of that began to fade in the 1980s as Reagan's trickle-down delusion was foisted on the American people like a poisonous candy bar. As more and more money was transferred out of the hands of the middle class and into the hands of a rich few, primarily by way of changes in tax policy, great wealth was accumulated by those who already had amassed huge amounts of money. Meanwhile, suffering increased among people competing for the ever-shrinking supply of resources dropped like crumbs from the table of the corporate elite.

Even that, however, was not the worst thing; the worst thing was the legitimization of greed that became a new cultural norm during that period—both a consequence of and a natural precursor to getting enough Americans to buy into the idea that those who hurt them most were those who were serving them best. Time and time again, people actually voted for those who spent their entire time as elected officials chipping away at the rights and opportunities that had allowed their own constituents to flourish. As the Supreme Court gave more and more permission to corporate forces of wealth and privilege to corrupt our political system, first Republicans and then, following closely behind, too many Democrats caught the wave of oligarchic enthusiasm. An orgy of privatization and deregulation made hundreds of people billionaires while it simultaneously turned millions of people into little more than economic serfs in their own country.

In time the Republican Party would be completely taken over by the oligarchic mentality, leaving high-minded conservatives almost homeless in their own party. Among Democrats, a not dissimilar process has been under way: while some lean into the corporatist mentality, progressives, the inheritors of the party's more traditional values, hold on by their fingernails in an effort to save the party from its oligarchic leanings. Although Democrats are still distinctly better than Republicans at actually standing for the good of the people, the two parties have become similarly beholden to corporate donors.

Economic and social injustice are not just about numbers on a page; they're about humanity. And I've been up close and personal with people whose lives have been affected deeply by the ravages of both. After a thirty-seven-year career in which I've seen the effects of unjust policies on the lives of men, women, and children throughout this country, I know how much potential is stunted and lives are limited by decisions made in far-off Washington by people who could simply couldn't care less. But I also know that these problems, as well as their root causes, lie deeper than the mere material plane on which they express themselves.

Underlying our economic crisis is a moral one, an ethical void that has allowed us to acquiesce to a system that has left so many tens of millions in deep despair. I was a huge Bernie Sanders supporter in 2016, as his agenda struck me at the time as the correct economic antidote to the corruption of our government by the donor class. But in the words of Albert Einstein, "We cannot solve our problems with the same thinking we used when we created them." It's time for a political conversation that addresses our problems both internally as well as externally, creating a more holistic and transformational approach to the problems in our midst.

A more integrative, whole-person, holistic perspective on how systems change is hardly new. It reflects a twenty-first-century mindset that now influences every corner of our society, from business to medicine, from education to psychotherapy and religion. Yet the political establishment seems not to have gotten that memo, and what I learned from running for president is that the system doesn't *want* to. Our political-media-industrial complex is a status quo that will not disrupt itself. Its power lies in maintaining the illusion that there is no real fundamental problem with the way we're doing things. Why? Because those who are handmaidens of the corporate plutocracy will go only so far in criticizing it. Theirs is a pre-prescribed conversation with a pre-prescribed group of candidates whom they deem qualified to stand in front of the American people as prospective leaders. Only those whose careers have not been entrenched in the system that got us into such a mess should be considered qualified to lead us out of it.

I learned the lengths to which the system will go to cast from its midst those who would question its underlying assumptions. Yet as a writer, I'm encouraged by the words of the Russian author Aleksandr Solzhenitsyn, "A writer is a government in exile." I'm so grateful to have the opportunity, as an author, to express things I feel most need to be expressed if America is to redeem herself.

*A Politics of Love* is a book I wrote to discuss ideas and

policies I believe we need to consider in order to transform our country. The book was written as a handbook to my presidential campaign. Since the book was first published, so much has occurred—from more devastation wrought by the chaos of the Trump presidency, to more racial upheaval, to the COVID-19 pandemic, to the insurrection on January 6, 2021. I have not added to the book's basic principles, however, as I feel they stand alone and remain legitimate. If anything, they presage the continuing horrors that have followed the book's publication, horrors that will continue to fester as wounds upon our body politic until we do what it takes to heal them.

There are no silver bullets or magical solutions that will heal America. To heal, we are going to have to dig deep—deep into our souls, deep into our history, and deep into the reasons why things have become as chaotic as they have. I hope this book will contribute to the conversations we need to be having, now and in the years ahead. America is in a state of moral and political decline, and we its citizens must commit to its repair on levels of effort that most of us have never summoned before. To fundamentally repair our country, we will need more than data; we will need courage, and we will need love.

Marianne Williamson, April 2021

# LOVE IN A TIME OF CRISIS
## LESSONS IN FEAR AND LOVE

I began lecturing on *A Course in Miracles*, a book of spiritual psychology, in 1983. I was thirty-one years old.

I was thrilled to have the opportunity to do what I loved: talking to others about the themes in a book that had made such a difference in my life. But I had no idea I was doing something that would become a career path. I simply thought I was talking about *A Course in Miracles* because it brought me joy to do it.

Then something happened. I was living in Los Angeles, and as anyone who was around at the time can testify, there began to be all this talk about a new, mysterious, very scary disease that was spreading. No one knew much about it except that it was deadly and communicable, mainly gay men were getting it, and there was no known cure. To contract it was an automatic death sentence. The disease was called AIDS.

I had been lecturing mainly to a small group of people at the Philosophical Research Society in the Los Feliz area, and suddenly my lecture audiences began to grow. We went from a small room on Saturday mornings to the auditorium on Tuesday nights, then from the auditorium on Tuesday nights to a church in Hollywood on both Tuesday nights and Saturday mornings. We continued to need more space. Gay men in Los Angeles—suddenly terrified—were looking for miracles, and with good reason.

Day after day, guests at someone's party turned into attendees at someone's funeral. Western medicine played various cards, but it was clearly stymied. In the early days of the epidemic it had nothing to offer, and organized religious institutions at the time were oddly quiet. One can see why a young woman talking about miracles, and about a God who loved everyone no matter what, was just the ticket for many. Most of my audience was young, and at the time I was too. None of us knew what had hit us, but my faith in miracles was strong and I was glad to share it.

Unless you've been in a war zone, you can't truly understand what those days were like. Friends and loved ones were dying all around us. Once people were diagnosed, there was apparently no hope for survival. People were young and gorgeous one day, then covered with horrible sores, blind, and walking with a cane the next. Many had to deal with the harrowing experience of revealing to their parents that they were gay *and* that they were dying. There was no room, and no time, for anything but being present to the moment, making every effort to survive. This wasn't the fun and fabulous eighties anymore. For many, life was lived on a razor's edge between life and death.

Everyone I knew was dealing with the disease, either directly because they had been diagnosed or indirectly because of friends or family who were. You were emotionally exposed to the epidemic simply by living in LA. The creative ranks of Hollywood contained a large gay population, and the entertainment community was hugely compassionate toward those who suffered. More and more people were being diagnosed who were *not* gay as well, having gotten the disease from blood transfusions, shared needles, or even one-night stands. The experience was overwhelming. To be alive at that time and in the presence of that disease was to be heartbroken—but it was also to be transformed. There is something about being around death that makes life more obviously precious.

Whatever shallow preoccupations might have meant something before meant nothing to us now. Superficial concerns simply melted away, except when needed as an escape valve. The goal was survival, by whatever means and for however long possible. And everyone was grasping for hope. I remember saying over and over, at lecture after lecture and support group after support group, "There doesn't have to be a cure for AIDS for it to become a chronic, manageable condition. There isn't a cure for diabetes, but it's a manageable condition!" We survived on that hope, articulating it over and over with tears in our eyes. I marvel at the fact that AIDS has now become, for many people, exactly that.

What I remember most from those days, however, is not the pain but the love.

I remember the people, both those who passed and those who remain. And like everyone who lived through that time, I remember so many stories. There was one young man named Merle, slightly built and shy, not the Hollywood type at all, who used to volunteer selling books at my lectures. As he grew ill, his father—built not at all like his son but more like a football quarterback—began helping him carry boxes of books to my lectures every Saturday morning. Merle's father was clearly unaccustomed to the world of gay Hollywood, and was at the very least in denial about his son's homosexuality. He sat at my lectures surveying the scene every Saturday, seeming to gradually awaken to what was happening around him. I would often watch him, so clearly flummoxed, so clearly heartbroken, as he did everything he could to help Merle continue an activity that gave meaning and purpose to his life.

Some today might find it hard to understand just how devastating it was for a young man at the time to be forced to deal not only with the disease, but with the fact that his parents didn't even know he was gay. Some expressed greater anxiety about saying, "Mom and Dad, I'm gay," than about saying, "Mom and Dad, I'm dying." Merle's father was someone for whom the idea of homosexuality was clearly foreign, but AIDS burst that closet door open for millions. Merle's father loved his son, and stood by him every step of the way; he also came to realize all the other gay men who were there for him too. And how that man transformed. On the day Merle died, both he and his father were surrounded by a community of gay men.

That story is one of millions of memories, not only mine but those of many others who were affected by the scourge of AIDS. I look back on that era now as having been a deep initiation, not just individually but collectively. Fear was there, horror was there, suffering was there. But love was there too.

Love was there in the people who were dying, and in the people who were there to try to help them die peacefully. Love was there in the support groups we held, the nonprofits we established, the arms with which we held each other, the hospitals where we visited each other, the acceptance with which we faced the death of so many, and the endless tears we cried and which I'm crying now as I write this.

I learned from that experience what tragedy looks like. But I also learned how beautiful people can be. To have learned those things on the level I learned them then is to know them in a way I could never forget. Whenever I meet someone I knew then, I feel a bond. We share something that did not go away when that period ended, something that would mark all of us forever. We lived through a crisis, yes. But in surviving it, we learned something very important: not only that crises pass, but that love is what gets us through them.

I have borne witness to many other crises since that time, both in my own life and in the lives of others. I've lived long enough to know, both personally and professionally, that there are seasons of life. As my father used to say, you take the good with the bad. From divorce and painful breakups to the deaths of loved ones to surviving abuse to professional and financial failures to serious illness—there are many ways that a life can fall, many variations of grief, and many forms that devastation can take. But one thing that makes suffering bearable is love. Love not only makes a crisis endurable; it makes it transformable. For where there is love, miracles happen. Love changes people, and when people are changed we change the world around us.

I have seen how love changes one life, but I have also seen how love changes groups of people. As someone who experienced the time of the Vietnam War with the attendant violence of the 1960s, and then the AIDs epidemic, I know what it feels like when groups of people experience a collective trauma.

———

In many ways, the political situation in America today seems like those times. Once again, there is an experience of shared chaos and anxiety. Our personal and political foundations seem as though they are under assault. But what feels to me to be lacking now is a sense that we are going through this crisis together. Too many seem to think today that their stress and anxiety is theirs alone, or at the least not deeply related to the stress and anxiety of others. The culture of self-centeredness that emerged in the 1980s and helped create this crisis to begin with now leaves us weakened in our capacity to deal with it. During Vietnam, the trauma was everyone's. During the AIDS crisis, the trauma was everyone's. But today, people are oddly cocooned in their misery. Many fail to realize either the collective reasons for our problems, or the collective changes necessary in order to solve them. Yet within the awareness of our oneness lie both our power to rise up and the ladder on which to climb. A belief in separation is always at the root of a problem, and a realization of our oneness is always at the root of its solution.

Self-love has become an odd sort of god in America. A generation that has become so sensitive to its own pain is often desensitized to the pain of others. One would think Jesus had come to earth to say, "Love yourself." Somewhere along the line, the "Love each other," "Love your neighbor as yourself" part has been subtly minimized, conveniently so for a market-based system that legitimizes self-centeredness as a lead-in to "I absolutely have to have this."

Any person, economic system, or political establishment that fails to concern itself with the pain of others is out of alignment with spiritual truth. And where there is a lack of spiritual alignment, chaos is inevitable. Spirituality is the path of the heart, and compassion for the human condition. Yet American politics has developed for decades in a direction that has had increasing disregard for such tender mercies. Hard data, hard facts, quantifiable factors are what's deemed to be real—serious, sophisticated, and relevant—making the separation of head from heart more justifiable and tenable. Material concerns matter, while spiritual concerns are deemed the stuff of fantasy. To the analytical mind, the journey of the soul seems irrelevant. And *that* is the beast. From there, we are lost.

The ego mind is very sly, and it's not a big leap from ignoring the pain of others to ignoring the fact that you yourself are inflicting pain on others. Once we give ourselves social permission to think that money, not love, is the organizing principle of a well-adjusted society, chaos is inevitable. And that is what has happened to us. The money of a few is given more attention than the pain of the many; the needs of those who are playing the game are deemed more important than the pain of the many left out of it. A phrase like "job loss" is a cold description, easily ignored after an hour's business meeting, for what is an experience of despair in the lives of millions.

Our political establishment was gobsmacked by the success of Donald Trump in the 2016 presidential election for exactly that reason. It didn't see it coming, but it should have. In its arrogant reliance on what it considers "hard facts," the political establishment failed to hear the galloping of a million hooves coming at it. And it didn't hear those hooves for one reason only: it wasn't listening. Psychological pain doesn't register on its radar. The chronic economic despair of millions of people—despair that our political establishment had in part created and largely failed to address—had been going on for years, and it was *going* to make itself heard in that election.

The political establishment was caught off guard because words like "despair," "anger," and "anxiety" refer to emotions, and the establishment mind-set sees emotions as "soft" rather than "hard" political factors. Its worldview is transactional rather than relational, treating the exchange of money far more seriously than the exchange of love. But a healthy political order does not leave our deep humanity out of the equation; it values the workings of the heart as well as the workings of the economy. Government is here to serve its people, and people are not just job numbers or cogs in a corporate machine. We are living, breathing, divinely created beings on this earth for a high and mighty purpose. No politics, and no political establishment, that fails to see us that way or treat us that way is worthy.

We don't just need a progressive politics or a conservative politics; we need a more deeply human politics. We need a politics of love. Love is the angel of our better nature, just as fear is the demon of the lower self. And it is love, not fear, that has made us great. When politics is used for loveless purposes, love and love alone can override it. It was love that abolished slavery, it was love that gave women suffrage, it was love that established civil rights, and it is love that we need now.

Fear has been politicized once again, and once again love must respond. Fear has been harnessed for political purposes, and the only thing powerful enough to override that fear is a harnessing of love. But love must be more than the reason we're doing something; it must also be the way we're doing it. Only nonviolent, spiritual resistance avoids the trap that is turning us into that which we resisted. Anger is like the white sugar of activist energy; it gives adrenaline in the short term but is debilitating in the long term. Love is the nutrition of the gods.

Where racism, bigotry, and hatred have been harnessed for political purposes, we need to harness love for political purposes. Where an economics without empathy or compassion has been harnessed for political purposes, we need to harness love for political purposes. Where the foundations of our democracy are being corroded by corruption, we need to harness love for political purposes. What is going on in America today is not just a political contest; it is a spiritual contest. Bigger forces are at work than mere political strategizing can cast from our midst. The darkest parts of the human psyche are seeking political expression, in America and around the world. Nothing short of a politics of love can drive them from our midst.

Over the last few decades, in keeping with the way pretty much everything else in America has been driven into a corporate straitjacket, American politics has been drained of its juice and turned into a rationalistic, abstract intellectual exercise based more on economic than human imperatives and invested more in dumbing down than in uplifting the American people. Our government has become a system of legalized bribery, less concerned with deep issues of humanity's purpose and more with shallow questions of money and power. This has put our politics squarely out of alignment with the evolutionary lure of this new century and the yearnings of the human heart.

People sense this, and a new wave of revolutionary fervor is rising up among us. It signals a new conversation out of which will emerge a new path forward. A fear-based, undemocratic influence has infected some of our most important institutions, and ancient thought forms of oppression and domination have reappeared among us. And we, like generations before us, are called upon to respond.

# Shaken Awake

Just as the body has an immune system, so does a society. Just as cells awaken to the need to heal an injured body, citizens awaken to the need to heal an injured group. No one had to tell anyone in New York City after the attacks of September 11, 2001, to show up to volunteer, to give blood, to help victims in any way they could. There is a deep instinctive yearning in all of us to create the good and repair the broken.

Several months ago, I was on an airplane when, just as it was gaining altitude after takeoff, a closet in the front flight attendant's cabin flew open. Food trays and drinks went everywhere, rolling down the aisle. What happened next was interesting. The hands of everyone sitting in an aisle seat just went to work, almost as though they were separate from the bodies they belonged to. The aisle was a sea of hands working together as though they had their own intelligence. Belonging to people who couldn't even see each other, one hand would pick up a can, pass it to someone else, and join with another to pick up a tray, all in a hugely smooth and successful operation that entailed no conversation whatsoever. No one messes around when there's a challenge on an airplane. If there's a job to do, you simply do it. And no one should mess around when there's a challenge to our democracy either.

The same biological intelligence at work in the physical immune system, the same emotional intelligence at work when responders came to the aid of victims after 9/11, and the same group intelligence at work on the airplane that day are available to us now should we choose to use them. We are going through a difficult time in America, and our political salvation lies in the arousal of a group intelligence.

For a country as for an individual, the issue is not just what we're going through, but also who we choose to be as we go through it. The same psychological, emotional, and spiritual dynamics that prevail in the life of one person prevail in the life of a group, because a nation is simply a collection of people. That's why those who understand what makes one life change are those who have a clue about how to change the world. Psychologists and philosophers know more about what's going on in America today than do traditional political strategists. And more important, in many cases they know more about what to do about it.

What is going on in our country is not just a political crisis, but a moral and a spiritual crisis as well. Our political challenges are mere symptoms of a deeper malaise and a deeper dysfunction. Humanity itself is being challenged to move on to the next stage of our evolution. If we try to solve our political problems only through traditional political means, the symptoms will merely morph into different forms. The only way we can deeply address our problems is if we are willing to address them on the level of cause.

The area of race is a specific example. As important as it was to abolish slavery, no stroke of a presidential pen or constitutional amendment could eradicate racism. What other generations changed on the outside, we need to also change on the inside. A politics of love is a holistic perspective on human change, addressing the internal as well as external aspects of societal dysfunction. Otherwise, ancient symptoms simply morph over time into new iterations.

Three tasks follow from our decision to apply spiritual wisdom to solving our political problems. First, we need to look the crisis squarely in the eye and take full responsibility for how we got here. Second, we need to atone for our mistakes as a nation and return to the democratic principles and universal human values from which we have strayed. Third, we need to realign our politics with the imperatives of love and humanitarian concern rather than the imperatives of short-term profit and power dictated by an amoral economic system.

In addition, we all need to take responsibility for the part we played as citizens in allowing our current upset to happen. As tempting as it is in life to blame everything on someone else, "other people" aren't always the problem. Our current political problems are like opportunistic infections that couldn't have taken hold unless we'd had a weakened societal immune system.

Our current problems did not come out of nowhere; in many ways, they're the inevitable consequence of compromises that we as citizens, in ways both large and small, made with the better angels of our nature over decades. As we neglected our civic responsibilities a little bit over here, disengaged from politics over there, allowed ourselves to be distracted by unimportant things over here, acquiesced to the diminishment of justice over there, compromised our values over here, and ignored a problem because it wasn't happening in our own neighborhood over there, slowly but surely our democracy began to experience serious distress.

It's easy to cast blame on others, but what's more helpful at this time is to take a deeper look at ourselves and our own issues: our distractedness, our belief that we are "too cool to care," our cynicism, our cultural superficiality, our denial, our lack of historical understanding, our insistence that "we aren't political." We the people have a problem, but at the deepest level we the people got ourselves into this ditch. And only we the people can get ourselves out of it.

Having won a world war for the cause of freedom in the mid–twentieth century, we didn't stop loving our freedom, but we began to take it for granted; we started tending to our money more than to our values, and we started protecting our egos more than our freedom. We became preoccupied with ourselves as individuals, concerned less with how to be good men and women and what it means to be a good society than with how to be rich and powerful. We were lured into a seductive web of lesser, self-centered goals, both as individuals and as a nation. We became reckless, irreverent, and irresponsible with too many things in too many ways. And now we are reaping what we have sown. The group naiveté of too many people thinking that "politics doesn't really matter," or that "other people are taking care of it," allowed a raging group pathology to develop.

Navigating this crisis will take not only the political renewal of our institutions but also some personal renewal of all of us. To reweave the rent fabric of our country, we're going to have to stitch it back together one torn place at a time. In order to grow from this collectively, we're going to have to grow from it individually. In the words of Martin Luther King Jr., we need "qualitative change in our souls as well as a quantitative change in our lives."

That we have serious challenges before us is true. And there is no reason to think that the assaults we're experiencing now will be lessening anytime soon. The very foundations of our democracy have been shaken, and we're in a situation we've not experienced in our lifetime. From threats to the press to assaults on equal treatment before the law, from economic policies that favor the wealth of a few over the health of people and planet to authoritarian behavior that runs counter to traditional democratic norms, many in power today have done more to undermine democratic governance than to exercise it. Our democracy itself is in peril now.

We're being reminded—painfully, and at a late hour—that democracy cannot be taken for granted. Perhaps we needed to get this close to the cliff for enough people to realize that we really don't want to fall over it. And often what shakes us to our core is what shakes us awake.

Americans have prevailed against threats to our democracy before, and we are going to do it again. From our earliest beginnings, there have been forces consistently ready to undermine the American experiment. Yet anyone who knows anything about American history knows that if Americans are sometimes slow to awaken to our problems, we slam it like nobody's business once we do.

We need, in our time, Lincoln's proverbial "new birth of freedom." Nothing less than that will override the forces that threaten us now. We need to take an evolutionary leap forward in how we think about ourselves and how we relate to each other; in what we think about America and how it relates to the rest of the world. We need to think deeply about our ancestors and more responsibly about our descendants. We need to awaken to the cries of children, to the cries of the desperate, and to the cries of the earth. We need a revolution of the heart.

It is not political mechanics but rather philosophical vision that will pull us back from the cliff and deliver us to sturdier ground. The power we need will emerge not from the identities that separate us but from the principles that unite us. One of our founding principles is *e pluribus unum*, or "unity in diversity," and as Americans we should cherish both. The level of our external separation is the level of our rich diversity, and that is a good thing. But what separates us physically need not divide us emotionally; what makes you different is not what should make you suspect. But now, in this moment of peril, we need to remember the universal principles that unite us as well. We need them to glue back the pieces of our fractured nation. We are white Americans and black Americans and brown Americans, Christian and Jewish and Muslim and atheistic Americans, gay and straight and transgender Americans, wild hipster Americans and staid traditional Americans, progressive Americans and conservative Americans. But we are all Americans. Every problem being experienced by any one group of Americans is rooted in the fact that we have strayed, as a nation, from the principles that apply to *all* Americans. To forget that freedom belongs to every American makes any American vulnerable. Whatever they can do to anyone they could someday do to you.

America's democratic values—that we are created equal; that we're given by God inalienable rights to life, liberty, and the pursuit of happiness; that governments are instituted to secure those rights—are the rock on which we stand. They come from the higher mind, and are the sacred calling of citizenship. More than any law or institution, those values are our only sure protection from tyranny. We need to rediscover them and fall in love with them again. It isn't enough that our values be inscribed on marble walls or on parchment. They must be inscribed in our hearts, generation after generation, or they lose their moral force. Only our love for them, and for each other, can unite us in a common field of devotion. From that field alone will we derive the power to endure and transform these difficult times.

# A New Politics

Our politics today is severely out of alignment with our decency, our love, and our higher intelligence—but we need to do more than just whine about that. We need to course-correct. We need to realign our politics with the angels of our better nature. We need to reclaim it for the best of who we are.

No one is doubting anymore that politics matters. What has happened in our country since the 2016 election makes political disengagement no longer an option for any serious person. We've learned the hard way the truth of the old French saying "If you don't do politics, politics will do you." Now we need to create a new political consciousness and drive it forward without delay.

Americans are not inherently a complacent people. It is in the characterological DNA of this country to push back against assaults on our freedom and to rise up when we have fallen down. The arrival of a new historical moment and the desire of the human heart to right the mistakes of the past: that was the original genesis of the country, and it's the psychological force we need to drive us forward now.

A person who lacks empathy or conscience is a sociopath. Similarly, an economic system that is essentially amoral—that does not factor empathy or conscience into its determination of right action—is a sociopathic economic system. When a government has become for all intents and purposes a mere handmaiden to such an economic system, democracy dies. Today, Americans are living at the behest of a tyrannous economic system that puts the short-term profit maximization of huge, multinational corporate entities before the health and well-begin of our people, the people of the world, and the planet on which we live.

Such is the crisis in which we find ourselves. Such is the crisis we must now transform.

This country was born in repudiation of tyranny, and we have shown at various times in our history that we have it in us to do it again. We have overthrown forces ranging from slavery to the oppression of women to Hitler's armies to institutionalized white supremacy, and more. Our ancestors were not sissies: when faced with forces of oppression, they said, "We can handle this." And then they did.

Most of the historical challenges to our freedom have taken the form of specific activities or institutions, like operable tumors that needed to be surgically removed. What confronts us now, however, is something more like a cancer that has already metastasized. What threatens our democracy today is an amoral economic worldview that puts money before love and things before people. It is an idolatrous mind-set that expresses itself in various ways through environmental, economic, and other forms of injustice that inevitably sacrifice the rights of people at an economic altar. The US government concerning itself more with the well-being of market forces than with the well-being of people and planet has created an untenable, unsustainable, and unsurvivable trajectory. We must interrupt it now.

The tyranny in America today is not really so different from the tyrannies of any other time or place; it's just branded better. A recurring pattern has merely repeated itself in a newer, softer, but no less pernicious form. An aristocratic archetype has waged its nefarious influence over us once again, luring us into willing acquiescence to a system in which the appetites of a few have gained precedence over the rights of the many.

That's why revolutionary political change is in the air. A democratic revolution can't be fought once, as in 1776, and then simply considered handled. Democracy is never safe from those who find it inconvenient to their purposes. Every generation has to rise up in its own time, face the challenges of its own day, and continue the revolution in its own way. The American Revolution is an ongoing process. In the words of President John F. Kennedy, "Those who make peaceful revolution impossible will make violent revolution inevitable."

Peaceful revolution is waged not with guns or bullets or violence, but with votes and consciousness and love.

A revolution is a new beginning. Today's cultural and political revolutionary needs to both think differently and act differently. Like a young person individuating from his or her parents, Americans need to ask ourselves what we will carry forward from the past, and what it's time to let go of. None of us, but particularly those who will live the majority of their lives (and for some of them, all of their lives) in the twenty-first century, should be burdened by outworn ideas left over from the twentieth. This is not a moment for obsolete formulas or for a mechanistic, externally obsessed twentieth-century mind-set that doesn't hold water in the twenty-first. The enlightenment of the twenty-first century represents a new perception of oneness among all aspects of our lives. This is the most powerful tool we have, not only for breaking free of what doesn't work anymore but for giving birth to what does.

Just as a body emerges from a physical womb, new ideas emerge from a womb of consciousness. It is from there, in our minds, that we can summon new possibilities for America and the world. We will re-create our country from the inside out, not by intellect or money or technology, but by the wisdom of the heart. A new politics will emerge from a new conversation, speaking to both external circumstances and deeper truths. We need to break free of the rationalism constraining our politics over the last few decades; such rationalism is too narrow to adequately describe our real problems or to adequately address them.

Life is deep, but our current politics is shallow. The history of this country is like the stuff of great art and philosophy, while our current politics is more on the level of gossip magazines. It is shallow and tawdry, an unworthy vehicle for grappling with the meaning of what we are going through. We need to think more deeply if we're to create more powerfully. We need to focus on a broader understanding of the American story and commit ourselves to rewriting it.

# Love and Fear

I n the spring of 2018, I visited Mauthausen, a former Nazi concentration camp in Austria. As I viewed the gas chambers that had been the vessels of industrialized mass murder and the ovens into which were cast the human remains of those killed, I witnessed the effects of Nazi hatred. During the Holocaust, the world saw what hatred and fear can do in their most wicked, evil form.

But I also saw at Mauthausen the plaque commemorating the American forces who liberated the camp at the end of the war. The Nazis were a horrifying example of collective darkness, but that darkness did not prevail. Allied forces won the war.

Ironically, while I was visiting the camp, the world watched in amazement as twelve little boys trapped in a cave in Thailand were saved in an extraordinary rescue mission. From the soccer coach who taught the boys meditation to help them remain calm and use less oxygen, to the divers and experts who gathered from all over the world to aid the Thai army efforts, the world saw that week what love can do. Whether emanating from people or emanating from nature, history gives us many examples of human tragedy and dysfunction. But it gives us examples of human transcendence as well.

From abolitionists, suffragettes, and civil rights activists here in America, to the international effort of the Allied forces during World War II and the team that rescued the boys in Thailand, the world has seen what happens when collective efforts dedicated to justice, peace, democracy, and love overcome forces that mitigate against them. History has shown what fear can do, but it has also shown us what love can do.

Nazis, white supremacists, and terrorist organizations of any stripe anywhere represent hatred harnessed for political purposes. And they are as potentially dangerous today as they have been at any other time. Such hate-filled groups do not represent—either in America or in the world at large—anything near a majority of the population. Yet they exert dark and increasingly dangerous influence.

The problem is not just that some people hate, however. The problem is that those who hate have a way of hating with conviction.

Conviction is a force-multiplier. I can't imagine a terrorist who's *kinda-sorta-sometimes-when-it's-convenient* committed to hate. Yet who among us has not at times been *kinda-sorta-sometimes-when-it's-convenient* committed to love? Hate has shouted, while too often love has only whispered. We need to display as much conviction behind our love as some have displayed behind their hate.

Sometimes the problem isn't that our commitment to love is shallow so much as that it's simply confined to the personal self. Many spiritual and religious groups in America still focus primarily on the role of love in the life of the individual. Nazis, white supremacists, and other such terrorists, however, are not just committed to hating an individual; they're committed to hating whole groups of people and effectuating social and political changes that reflect that hate. That is why we need a politics of love. We need to commit to loving humanity, and effectuate social and political changes that reflect our love.

Love is the core of nonviolent political philosophy as articulated by Mahatma Gandhi, who argued that love would heal our political relationships as well as our personal ones. Dr. Martin Luther King Jr. traveled to India and brought back Gandhi's principles of nonviolence to apply to the struggle for civil rights in the American South in the 1960s. Gandhi and King turned love into a broad-scale social force for good. And what they did in their time, now we need to do in ours.

The love that will save the world is not only a love for our own children, but a love for everyone's children. And it isn't just a desire to save our own homes; it's a realization that this planet is everyone's home. A politics of love sees the world through reverent eyes, viewing love, not economics, as the most enlightened organizing principle for human civilization. This view represents a fundamental change in our human, political, and economic priorities—not merely an incremental approach to bettering society.

In the words of the French philosopher Teilhard de Chardin, "Someday, after mastering the winds, the waves, the tides and gravity, we shall harness for God the energies of love, and then, for a second time in the history of the world, man will have discovered fire." I used to read those words and think it would be nice if it were to happen. Now I read them and realize that *only* if it happens will humanity survive.

It's not naive to suggest that we reorient our politics around love's purposes. What's naive is to think that we can afford *not to,* and retain either our freedom or our survival as a species. When fear has coalesced into a terrible sickness, the only medicine is love. A worldview centered on love is no less sophisticated or psychologically astute than any other—in fact, it is more sophisticated than any other. It is the only worldview that nurtures and sustains life.

Responsibility means *response-ability*. Fear is speaking loudly in the world today; now we the people need to respond.

## "Fight the System, Little Sister"

Years ago, I mentioned to a friend that I noticed children weren't saying the Pledge of Allegiance like we used to do, and I wondered why.

He practically yelled in my ear. "Because there *is* no f—kin' liberty and justice for all in this country, man! That's why!!"

"Yes," I said. "But the fact that when I was a little girl I put my hand over my heart and pledged allegiance to one nation, under God, with liberty and justice for all, turned me into a woman who gets really upset when I see liberty and justice not happening."

The Pledge of Allegiance is not a guarantee; it is a *pledge*. The fact that our country at times has so veered so far away from "liberty and justice for all"—indeed, that we have never fully actualized that reality for all our citizens, and in many ways are veering from it now—is a call to awaken, not to whine. No earlier generation *owed* us anything, and many of them contributed mightily to the lives we live today. Sometimes this country has gotten it right, and sometimes we have gotten it wrong. But cynicism about our history on the Left is no less revisionist than denial about our history on the Right. The world has never been perfect, but our job is to make it better now. As an old rabbinical saying goes, "You are not expected to complete the task, but neither are you allowed to abandon it."

When I was growing up, the one thing that was never allowed in our house was whining. We were told that if we had a challenge, we had to rise to it. And where the world was broken, it was our job to repair it.

My father grew up in deep poverty and was very sensitive to issues of social justice. He knew what it meant to be poor, he knew what it meant to be hungry, and he knew how large and powerful systems can keep such misery in place. Throughout my childhood, a constant refrain was "Fight the system, kids! Fight the system!"

Everyone in the family knew what he meant by that. "The system" is not just a particular political or economic structure, but a morally corrupt way of looking at the world—a loveless mind-set externalized in material form. It is the social, political, and economic expression of a worldview that says, "I matter, but you don't. My gain matters, but your suffering doesn't. Whoever might be hurting, it's someone else's problem." It is a political order devoid of the sense that we are our brother's keeper, that what we do to others will be done to us, or that our mission here is to love others as we would wish to be loved.

Often, when passing an elderly janitor cleaning a building late at night or a homeless person begging on the street, my father would say to us, "See that old man, kids? *His life is hard*." He would quote Linda in Arthur Miller's *Death of a Salesman* saying to her sons about their father, Willie, "Attention must be paid." Too often, when it comes to the suffering of others, we look but we do not see.

When I became an adult and began to write and speak about spirituality, my father at first seemed to think I'd betrayed his values. He had taught me about society at large, and he could not understand my focus on personal transformation. "I raised you to fight the system, to wage the revolution!" he exclaimed to me one day.

I replied, "But, Daddy, I am! Love *is* the revolution! It's the only way that things will fundamentally change."

I saw a twinkle in my father's eye when I said that. He did understand. One of my most precious memories is walking into my parents' bathroom one day when my father was shaving. He was listening to one of the early cassette tapes of my lectures, and as I entered the room he turned to me, put down his razor for a moment, and said, "Very good, Little Sister. I'm proud of you." Today, twenty years after my father's death, I feel at times like I'm still trying to get his approval.

Over the years, I have gone from having to justify my spiritual interests to a politically oriented father to feeling the need to justify my political interests to a spiritually oriented audience. After the 1960s, those two domains—politics and spirituality—had taken differing directions, and I felt caught between the two. I had been comfortable during the time when we read Ram Dass in the morning and went to antiwar rallies in the afternoon. That creative mix fit my temperament then and fits my temperament now. Spirituality is simply the path of the heart, and if it applies to anything, then it applies to everything.

A few years ago, a young man said to me at one of my lectures, "But aren't you kind of an aging hippie, Ms. Williamson? Your generation was just into sex, drugs, and rock 'n' roll!" I replied with a knowing smile: "Uh . . . that was just *part* of the day!!" Then I was silent for a moment. "We spent the rest of the day stopping a war."

I knew he heard me. The revolution of my youth occurred on both inner and outer planes. It was sex, it was culture, it was music, *and* it was politics. The spirit of rebellion today feels similar in that it isn't confined to any one category; rather, its influence is everywhere. Love's revolutionaries aren't antiestablishment now; more enlightened thinkers *are* the new establishment.

Should we allow our internal wisdom to guide us as much as an exterior road map, then a divine intelligence will show each of us the part we can play in the creation of a new America. This moment is not just a time of breakdown; it is also a time of breakthrough. Millions of Americans are doing the

heavy lifting all over the country, both electorally and nonelec-
torally, dealing with our challenges creatively and making us,
despite the difficulty of this moment, an even better nation for
what we are going through. Our current unrest can lead to a
national reset if we're willing to become the people we need to
be in order to do the things we need to do.

America has fallen, and now it's time for us to rise.

# 2

# A REVOLUTION OF LOVE
## REVIEWING THE PLOT

You can't pick up a novel in the middle of the book and have any idea what's going on. You don't know the characters and you don't know the plot. You need to read it from the beginning to know how the story unfolds.

The same is true with the story of a nation. We can't really understand what's going on in this country without understanding where we've come from. We can't recognize forces for what they represent historically when all we can see is how they relate to us now. With almost every issue, what happens now is part of a continuing narrative that began over two hundred years ago. Issues erupting dramatically today have been developing for years, often underneath the surface, as generation after generation writes its chapter in our ongoing history.

Whether you're learning the history of your family or the history of your ethnic group or religion, knowing where you come from gives you a clue into who you are. It's difficult to understand what it means to be an American today without understanding what America means, period.

Yet what America means is open to interpretation. To some people, America means a bright spot of freedom and liberty whose shadows and mistakes are secondary to the exceptionalism of our first principles. To them, our country is so good that it hardly matters what we've done wrong. To others, it seems America's historical errors justify perpetual condemnation. To them, at times we've been so bad that it hardly matters what we've ever done right. We won't be led through the storm of this moment, either by those who love this country blindly or by those who condemn her blindly. For the blind cannot see.

The guiding light of America's destiny is neither blind to our problems nor blind to our potential. We will be led through our current storm by the inner light of a more sophisticated, compassionate understanding that America is a continuing narrative. Like any of us, it isn't a finished product yet. Nor will it ever be. A nation is continuously moving through time, like a novel whose ending can't be foreseen. What we need now is a deeper understanding of what came before, and a deeper commitment among us to write well the chapter that is ours.

Today, we seem tethered neither to where we came from nor to where we wish to be going. We've lost the plot of our democracy—we're not connecting the dots, and we're not connecting the dots because we're not connecting the facts. We're not connecting the facts because the facts have been scrambled.

Our founders sought safeguards against such scrambling, but the safeguards have been weakened. Thomas Jefferson wanted free public education because only people whose critical thought processes had been honed could be entrusted with the power of self-governance. And he wanted a free press to make sure all citizens had the information we would need in order to make wise decisions. If you're entrusted with the power to direct a country—which, in a representative democracy, we the people are—then you need to be educated in order to know how to think, and informed by a free press in order to know what to think. On both fronts, however, our power has been diminished.

Someone knew exactly what they were doing when American civics and history lessons started disappearing from many public school curricula. In eleven states, there is no required civics or American history education at all. In more than half of them, no more than half a year learning those subjects is required. But if someone didn't learn about the Bill of Rights when they were a child, how would they know to be appalled as an adult when they see it under assault?

Knowledge is power, and withholding knowledge is a tool of all oppressive systems. Underresourcing education, particularly among children, and corporate consolidation of the news media have been powerful tools in the dumbing down of the American mind. Without an informed and passionate citizenry, democracy is not a problem for its enemies at all.

Giving people a lot of consumer products but not giving them information is like giving people lots of candy but withholding basic nourishment. Perhaps if you give people a way to make more money, they won't notice that you've taken away something even more precious. If you legitimize their self-centeredness, they'll be more likely to forget about their ancestors, their fellow citizens, or their descendants.

One of the most powerful things an American citizen can do today is read up on American history, a lot of which most of us don't remember from school and many of us never even learned. There are enough "American History for Dummies"–type books out there that no one really has much of an excuse for not brushing up on our nation's history. We gain a deeper understanding of the present when we have a context that includes the past, and a deeper understanding of who *we* are when we know who came before.

The more we understand the larger narrative of our history and the chapters that were written by other generations, the more empowered we are in writing our own. We learn, among other things, that many of the forces we're dealing with now are simply the latest iterations of challenges that have been with us from the beginning. The current crisis in our country is the continuation of a narrative that began over two hundred years ago.

The first historical through-line is our foundational democratic principles, the values on which we purport to stand. Inscribed in our Declaration of Independence in 1776, these first principles are the light that guides us through every travail: that all men are created equal; that God gave all men unalienable rights to life, liberty, and the pursuit of happiness; and that governments are instituted to secure those rights. Along with those unalienable rights go freedom of speech, freedom of the press, the right to bear arms, freedom of peaceful assembly, freedom to protest, and several more meant to ensure our ability to remain a free people. Another fundamental American principle was articulated by Abraham Lincoln in the Gettysburg Address: that "government of the people, by the people, and for the people, shall not perish from the earth."

Those ideas are not just abstract concepts. They are living, breathing forces for which hundreds of thousands of people have struggled, lived, and died. Every one of them represents a freedom in the absence of which every American would live a very different life.

But a second through-line has also been with us from the beginning, and that is a fierce resistance to those first principles on the part of those who see them as threatening to their interests. Usually, though not always, such forces represent the economic interests of the few pitted against the interests of the many.

So on one hand, we're a nation "conceived in liberty"; on the other hand, our entire Southern economy was based on the slave trade and it took the Civil War to end it. On the one hand, we believe in the "unalienable rights to life, liberty, and the pursuit of happiness"; on the other hand, we perpetrated the genocide, forced migration, and cultural annihilation on the Native peoples of this continent. On the one hand, we believe that "all men are created equal"; on the other hand, institutionalized white supremacy and segregation raged throughout the South for a hundred years even after the end of the Civil War. That dichotomy represents a dramatic, often tragic pattern that has been with us from the beginning: we were founded on enlightened principles, have in many ways ourselves been the most violent perpetrators against them, and then ultimately—at least most of the time—have reclaimed them.

Slavery was met with abolition, suppression of women was met with the suffragette movement, segregation was met with the civil rights movement, and so forth. Every generation of Americans has included both enemies of democracy and heroes of democracy. Our generation is even now in the midst of deciding which one, in our time, will prevail.

Political manifestations, both good and bad, are but outer reflections of internal realities. They emerge from realms beyond what the eye can see. Love and lovelessness are constantly duking it out, in our hearts and in our world. Slavery, oppression, racism, and so forth are more than mere political wrongs; they represent spiritual malfunctions. Until we deal with our problems on the level from which they emerge, then no matter what we do to solve them, they will simply morph into other forms. Whether it is a health problem or a money problem or a relationship problem or a political problem, both the source of any problem and the source of its solution lie within our consciousness.

That is why a new American revolution is a revolution of consciousness, and a new American politics is a politics of love. If the choice to love remains merely a private decision, then it will have only private effects. Only when love is applied to public issues will it then have public effects.

An overly secularized, rationalistic politics is an inadequate response to the challenges of our time. A politics of love is a twenty-first-century, whole-person politics that speaks to both external and internal issues.

External activism fosters a different way of doing things, which is important. But internal activism fosters a different way of thinking about those things as well. Both are important, because everything we do is infused with the consciousness with which we do it. In the words of Mahatma Gandhi, "The end is inherent in the means." Enlightenment is a shift in worldview, and only a more enlightened thinking can deliver us to an enlightened world.

America's founders were products of the eighteenth-century Enlightenment, or Age of Reason, during which Western civilization overthrew the mystification of early church dogma in favor of rational thought and individual freedom. Today, we are entering a new Era of Enlightenment, in which we are overthrowing the limits of overly rationalistic thinking that doesn't recognize the powers of the soul. We are evolving beyond a twentieth-century worldview that posited the world as one big machine, and realizing that in fact it is more like one big thought. Consciousness is no longer deemed irrelevant to human affairs, but rather the driver of human affairs. Things in the outer world are merely effects created by thoughts we think. The role of consciousness in transforming events is the essential realization of a twenty-first-century worldview. Only if we rethink the world will we be able to re-create it. Only in transforming our hearts will we be able to transform the world.

A political mind-set mired in twentieth-century thinking is incapable of solving our most pressing problems, because its focus on externalities too often leaves their causes unaddressed. It waters the leaves but not the roots of our democracy. Not every force that is driving our world is visible to the physical eye. A politics that gives little credence to the inner life, considering it outside the purview of its analysis, is inadequate to the task of navigating these difficult times.

That is why the spiritual seeker is important to the transformation of our politics, and of our country. Spiritual seekers have always been the harbingers of political change in America—the abolitionist movement was started by the early Evangelicals and Quakers, and the civil rights movement was led by a Baptist preacher. Jews and Catholics have been central to the unfoldment of every social justice movement throughout our history.

In the words of Plato, "To philosophize and do politics are one and the same thing." Not only does enlightened politics require spiritual understanding, but enlightened spirituality requires attention to politics. No serious religious path gives anyone a pass on addressing the suffering of other sentient beings. The idea that we can leave politics out of our conceptualization of our spiritual journey is an outdated concept, because politics is simply the journey we take together. We can't transform our country without transforming our politics, and that we can do only by participating. Standing on the sidelines is not an option for a conscious seeker, or for a conscious citizen. Too much blood and too much suffering result from an unconscious politics for those of us who claim to be on the journey of higher consciousness to ignore. We must take a fundamental step forward in re-creating the world from the inside out.

"Love each other" is not just a prescription for personal salvation; it is a prescription for political renewal as well.

When tens of millions of people trapped in economic shackles with little dignity, few prospects, and little hope are then told by a political candidate that the system is rigged against them and only he can fix it, you can't just blame the candidate for taking advantage of all that hopelessness. The larger responsibility lies with a political establishment that allowed such mass despair to develop in the first place—and with those of us who allowed it to.

Economic despair is not a statistic in the lives of people who are living with it; it is a real, devastating human experience. It is a festering wound from which other symptoms emanate, such as domestic violence, opioid addiction, sickness, bad health from lack of access to care, depression, suicide, and a general breakdown of community and culture.

In a country dominated by a political system that has been dedicated more to its campaign donors than to its people, and more to the financial gain of the wealthy .01 percent of its population than to the actual practice of democracy, the crisis we now have on our hands was almost inevitable. A massive cry of economic despair was going to make itself heard—whether in support of a progressive populist such as Bernie Sanders, or an authoritarian populist such as Donald Trump. It's not that either of them necessarily had better plans for dealing with all that suffering than did Hillary Clinton; it's just that they're the only two candidates who *acknowledged* all that suffering. And that made all the difference.

Having substituted obeisance to the dictates of market forces for obeisance to the dictates of democratic and humanitarian concerns, the political establishment is reaping now what it has sowed. Climate change has reached extreme and dangerous levels because the US government has done more to advocate for the short-term maximization of profits to the fossil fuel and chemical companies than to advocate for the well-being of our citizens and our planet; our tax policies do more to fill the coffers of the 1 percent than to address the economic struggles of the 99 percent; and our efforts to protect national security center on increased preparedness for war yet diminished efforts at waging long-term peace. All of those factors represent more than a political challenge; they represent dire threats, over the long run, to our democracy and quite possibly to the very existence of our species.

Such problems represent something deeper and more fundamental than a system dedicated to externalities has any idea how to fix. They are reflections of the fact that, in the words of Gandhi, "humanity is not in its right mind."

A lack of love is the level of the problem, and a lack of love is the level of the solution. Only when we realign our politics with our deep universal values will the forces arrayed against us fade away. In the words of Albert Einstein, "The problems of the world will not be solved on the level of thinking we were at when we created them."

Political issues are *moral* issues. War and peace are moral issues. Economic injustice is a moral issue. Mass incarceration is a moral issue. Unfair tax laws are a moral issue. Racial inequality is a moral issue. Breaking treaties with Native tribes is a moral issue. The neglect of America's children is a moral issue. Global poverty is a moral issue. A self-perpetuating war machine is a moral issue. Putting immigrants in cages is a moral issue.

The question is not simply what we should *do* about such problems. The larger question is, *Who are we* that such problems even exist among us? And who do we have to become in order to solve them?

Whether for an individual or for a nation, every crisis comes with two things: a reflection of who we have been, and an invitation to become who we need to become. And that is where America is now. We need to reach for higher ground than that on which we've been standing over the last few decades. Nothing less will heal our country.

Separating politics from the deeper questions of our humanity leaves us dangerously fractured as a civilization. America needs to atone for some mistakes of our past and make serious amends. We need to be willing to do things differently moving forward. And we need to take a brutally honest look at how certain concepts left over from the late twentieth century do more to corrode than to advance our democracy. A new kind of American—a new kind of thinker and a new kind of citizen—needs to arise now.

And quickly.

# We the People, We the Problem

For too many decades, Americans have been chronically distracted by less important things, not bothering to engage in serious self-examination. Material progress has become our false god.

While private morality might have thrived among individuals, issues of public morality began to wither. Economic values have taken precedence over ethical values, and now we're having to face the consequences of this moral corrosion. An amoral economic system, in which a corporate bottom line is given precedence by our government over considerations of who or what gets hurt, has corroded our nation's politics. And the symptoms are everywhere. Wealth inequality, racial and criminal injustice, the undue influence of money on our government, the desecration of our environment, the destruction of nonindustrial farming, compromised food and water supplies, opioid addiction, lack of educational and economic opportunity for the many while a tiny few are made richer every day—all were wounds given a chance to fester while too many of us weren't looking, weren't even complaining about the problem if it didn't apply to us.

Politicians who tried to warn us of what was happening were typically viewed as "too negative," and journalists whose job is to inform us about what's happening were too often owned by the very forces that drove this systematic selling-off of our collective good. Once a few corporate conglomerates were allowed to own the majority of our news outlets (i.e., the term *corporate media*), stories that once might have earned someone a Pulitzer for good investigative journalism began just as likely to get the journalist fired.

The main organizing principle of American society today is not democracy; it is short-term profit maximization of multinational corporations. Our government does not now function to protect its citizens from overreach by corporations, so much as it works to protect corporations from all those pesky citizens who keep demanding that their rights be respected.

Democracy is not the enemy of an amoral economic system; it's simply *inconvenient* to an amoral economic system. The thieves who stole the treasures of our democracy—a thriving middle class, accessible health care, a robust educational system, and proper environmental stewardship—didn't use brute force to knock down the door. No, they used the soft, insidious power of political propaganda that no seriously thinking person should have fallen for. Yet too many of us were not serious. Too many of us were not thinking. The American people have been played for fools.

As early as the 1980s, the causes of many of our deepest problems were sold as good economic policy. Plans were laid for an economic reversion to what is basically an aristocratic system; "trickle-down economics" hailed as our economic salvation when in fact it created all manner of entitlement for the few and all manner of misery for the many. It did not uplift our middle class; quite to the contrary, it destroyed our middle class: from workers losing their jobs when corporations got tax breaks for moving their factories overseas to farmers being pushed off their land so agribusiness could take over to mental health care facilities being closed all over the country to attacks on unions, stealing from the middle class in order to give more to the rich was actually sold as good economic policy. Over and over we've elected those whose policies exalt the profits of corporations over the well-being of our citizens. Just enough of the serfs were allowed to get rich themselves, you see. What a clever sleight of hand prevailed.

The wealth inequality in America today has led to what is essentially a new class of aristocrats and a new class of serfs. In the richest nation on earth, roughly 40 percent of our citizens now have a hard time covering their basic costs, from food and health care to transportation and rent. Sixty-two percent of Americans cannot be deemed members of the middle class. Millions of Americans have to work at two or three low-wage jobs just to make ends meet. And in issues ranging from justice to education to health care to environmental protection, the underlying cancer of unbridled corporate influence on political campaigns is poisoning the very roots of our democracy.

In the words of the late Supreme Court justice Louis Brandeis, "We may have democracy, or we may have wealth concentrated in the hands of a few, but we cannot have both."

The "few" in this context are made up mainly of large corporate interests, for whom government now, for all intents and purposes, primarily functions. Their flood of undue financial influence—especially since the Supreme Court *Citizens United* decision removed restrictions on their donations to campaign coffers—is now so great as to chronically and systematically override the will of the American people. Author Jane Mayer refers to this nefarious phenomenon as "dark money."

Like addicts coming out of denial, no longer thinking that they can control their drinking or drugging, Americans need to get out of our denial regarding the depth of corruption that prevails within our political establishment. Such a moment of clarity can be frightening at first, but it's also a moment when breakthroughs occur. It opens the mind to the possibility that there might be another way. And there *is* another way. That way is not to disparage our democracy, but to reclaim it, rebuild it, and return it to its deepest principles. It is ultimately our emotional connection to democracy, and our devotion to the possibilities it creates for the human race, that will empower us to save it.

Democracy is important because it is a conduit for the will and the wisdom of the people ourselves. If we lose sight of that internal value, then we lose the light that guides us. And that light is not mere symbol; it is the power of enlightened thought. "Through the night with the light from above" from the song "God Bless America" is not just a lyrical phrase. America is experiencing a dark night of the soul now, and we need our light—our wisdom, and our love—to guide us. For in the words of Abraham Lincoln, "We shall nobly save, or meanly lose, the last best hope of earth."

# Reclaiming Our Revolutionary Spirit

The United States was born of the courage and commitment to start something new. We're always starting new things, whether it's new projects, new businesses, or new versions of ourselves. That is an upside to who we are.

The very founding of our country established a new possibility for humanity, repudiating an aristocratic system and starting over on an entirely new philosophical foundation. To Europeans at the time, we were called "the New World."

The Old World was based on social inequality, and the New World, at least in theory, was to be based on social equality. The very idea of such a radical departure from the past was revolutionary. In the words of Thomas Paine in 1776, "We have it in our power to begin the world over again."

According to an ancient monarchical system, a king, a queen, and their cronies, the aristocracy, had been deemed entitled to land, education, wealth, wealth-creation, and all other means necessary to actualize their dreams. No one else was so entitled. No one else could own land, get an education, or create wealth for themselves. An aristocratic system gave power to those at the top—and only those at the top—to be shared with those below only at their will. According to "the divine right of kings," God shared His power only with a king, who could then use the power to lord over people at will.

With the founding of the United States, God wasn't seen to have given power to a king with which to rule over us; He was seen to have given power to the people with which to govern ourselves. Governments were established to secure our rights, and we were given constitutional authority to redress our government if it failed to do so.

That's why the very notion that all men are created equal was—and remains—so radical. An entirely new political possibility emerged from the *idea* of equality. The American Dream has never been a fully actualized reality; forty-one signers of the Declaration of Independence themselves owned slaves. But the power of the American Dream lies in the power of a *possibility*, a possibility never yet fully embodied on the material plane, but one that has lived on in the imagination, hopes, and aspirations of generation after generation.

When the behavior of our government is out of sync with the rights of the American people, then it's in the finest American tradition to protest our government and seek redress. American citizens aren't here to be good boys and girls, to do as we're told, to just go along to get along. We were born of an audacious spirit, and that audacity runs in our veins even now.

We were founded by revolution, and have been sustained by minirevolutions ever since. And now it is time for another one. It is our responsibility, to ourselves and to our children, to cast off any chains of an economic tyranny. An economic system that is predicated on the notion that giving more to the rich somehow helps the poor (contrary to all evidence, by the way) is as tyrannous as the aristocracies of old. The fact that the new aristocrats wear pin-striped suits and are often highly educated doesn't make the system less tyrannous; it just makes it more familiar. In the words of Thomas Paine, "A long habit of not thinking a thing wrong gives it a superficial appearance of being right." But it isn't right. It is *wrong*.

For decades, we have made the short-term financial gain of corporations—slowly and incrementally at first and ultimately in a huge cascade of democracy-demolishing economic tsunamis— the false god of our day, the idol of our imagination, and the master of our destiny. That is the issue underlying almost every other issue, from endless wars to environmental desecration to economic hardship to a lack of health care and inadequate child care. There is no one to blame so much as something to take responsibility for, a fact to realize, a dream from which to awaken, and actions to take while there is still time.

Whether it's a king lording over us or a corporate donor class exerting undue influence on our government—the economic equivalent of lording over us—the right and responsibility of every generation of Americans is to cast off any chains that bind us.

The moral mission of the United States is to create a society in which, to the best of our ability, all material shackles are removed that keep any person from becoming who he or she was created to be. It is every generation's task to claim that mission, and to further it. The power of our first principles, our democratic values, is that they speak to something higher than politics. They speak to the human condition.

America's higher purpose is not just to allow you to have what you want, or to allow me to have what I want. Our higher purpose is to give everyone a fair shot at making their dreams come true. Anything that stands in the way of that will ultimately deprive all of us of the opportunities we hold most dear. For America doesn't belong to any one of us; America belongs to all of us.

That kind of thinking was radical in 1776, and it's radical today.

It's radical to declare that God created all men equal.

It's radical to declare that God gave all of us unalienable rights to life, liberty, and the pursuit of happiness.

It's radical to insist that governments are instituted to secure and protect those rights.

And it's radical to insist that our government should be a government "of the people, by the people, and for the people."

Such philosophical radicalism is our heritage, but it cannot be guaranteed. Once a democracy is established, it cannot be taken for granted. Just as a relationship must be tended to, and our bodies must be tended to, and our careers must be tended to in order to thrive, so our democracy must be tended to. Its survival isn't guaranteed. At what point in a flight, once a plane is in the air, can the pilots then afford to ignore the panels in the cockpit? Every citizen is a pilot of our democracy, and if we do not think of ourselves that way, and act that way, then the plane of our democracy goes down.

Devotion to the ideal of democracy is a living force; it needs to be kept alive in our hearts and fostered by our political engagement. Democracy does not drive itself.

As Thomas Jefferson wrote to James Madison in 1787: "I hold it that a little rebellion, now and then, is a good thing, and as necessary in the political world as storms in the physical." We rebelled against the tyrannies of slavery, female oppression, and segregation. We rebelled against monopolies and purveyors of child labor. We rebelled against union busters and dangerous work environments. We don't need to summon up some new revolutionary spirit now so much as claim the one that has always been part of us.

Americans remain a rebellious people, but too often our rebellion is misplaced. We expend our spirit of rebellion on relatively minor matters, like a cable company denying us the premium package, rather than on confronting the unholy alliance of government and corporate tyranny. This has got to change, or we will lose something very precious.

Neither the exceptionalism of our principles nor liberty itself can be automatically bequeathed from parents to children. They must be won and rewon with every generation. No amount of money, political strategizing, or algorithms can substitute for the emotional power expressed by enough people who really care. And that is what the new revolution of consciousness signifies: millions of Americans are now realizing—many for the first time—that when it comes to what happens to our democracy, we really do care.

There has been a stirring of democratic fervor in the United States over the past few years, making it clear that we do: the Tea Party, the Women's Marches, activism led by students after the mass shooting in Parkland, Florida, uproar over the separation of families at our southern border, and the resistance movement" since the 2016 election. We indeed are heirs to revolutionary forefathers, and at last we are beginning to act that way. Now, at arguably the eleventh hour, a generation that had been on the verge of amusing itself to death has awakened to the fact that there is nothing amusing at all about the death of our democracy.

# The Reawakening

A spiritual awakening is necessary to redeem our country, but a spiritual awakening takes courage. And a spiritual awakening takes love.

Some Americans have a hard time loving this country today because they're ambivalent about things that occurred in the past—and even some things occurring in the present that we haven't taken responsibility for. Without a willingness as a nation to become more self-aware, we will not be spiritually awakened. And we will not be able to summon up the emotional and psychological strength to take us to a better place.

It's important that we recognize America's historical errors, not as a reason for national self-hatred, but as a foundation for correcting them. It's true that this country has committed atrocities, from slavery to the genocide of Native Americans to the oppression of women to institutionalized white supremacy to violently enforced segregation to the cruelty of separating parents from their children at our Southern border. But we have also seen the rise—and the success—of the abolitionist movement, the women's suffrage movement, the civil rights movement, the marriage equality movement, and so forth. We should identify our problems, but identify *with* the problem-solvers. We have always embodied a characterological struggle between the most illumined principles and the basest human instincts; that is nothing new. But our historical narrative has been one of ultimately improving things. And cynicism is just an excuse for not helping.

We're both a brilliant country and a country that has made some terrible mistakes. But our pattern has been one in which enough Americans rise up in their time, with power and love for the possibilities they know in their hearts are real, to *right* those wrongs. The problem-solvers of our past didn't act like victims— they proclaimed victory and saw it through. And so can we. They didn't just sit around and make cynical comments, or complain about their exhaustion, or simply yell at those who disagreed with them. Transformational love requires personal maturity. It is convicted and fierce, and so should be our politics. We're not the first generation to be compelled to push back against antidemocratic forces. Let's just make sure we're not the first one to fail.

But we will fail if we keep having the same conversation we've been having for the last forty years—and doing the same things we've been doing for forty years—but pretend things will turn out differently. We must move into a higher level of awareness in order to interrupt the patterns of crisis, for the laws of consciousness are set and unalterable. Merely tinkering with the external effects of our problems will not be enough to solve them. Fear destroys and love creates. An amoral economic system cannot not produce chaos, and love cannot not produce miracles.

The choice is between chaos and miracles. And the choice is ours.

Again the words of Jefferson:

> *I am not an advocate for frequent changes in laws and constitutions, but laws and institutions must go hand in hand with the progress of the human mind. As that becomes more developed, more enlightened, as new discoveries are made, new truths discovered and manners and opinions change, with the change of circumstances, institutions must advance also to keep pace with the times. We might as well require a man to wear still the coat which fitted him when a boy as civilized society to remain ever under the regimen of their barbarous ancestors.* [*]

Now, in the twenty-first century, we must once again keep pace with the times. We need to align ourselves politically with "the progress of the human mind" that marks the realizations of the times in which we live. With a more whole-person approach to everything from health to relationships, we *have* become more developed and we *have* become more enlightened. The biggest problem we have collectively is that our politics lag behind.

---

[*] *The Papers of Thomas Jefferson,* edited by J. Jefferson Looney, Retirement Series (Princeton, NJ: Princeton Univ. Press, 2004), 9:151.

Our political establishment, too often at the behest of its corporate overlords, cannot but deliver the spawn of its malfeasance. Yet we continue to expect that those who knew how to do things before are somehow the ones who know how to do things now—even when things that they did before were spectacular failures.

Someone who led you into a ditch isn't usually the one who knows how to lead you out of it. So why do we keep looking backwards? "Seasoned politicians" led us into wars in Vietnam and Iraq; "seasoned politicians" created the biggest wealth inequality since 1929; "seasoned politicians" brought us to the brink of environmental catastrophe. Clearly, we need a new kind of seasoning.

Our politics, and our political establishment, remain in the coat that Jefferson referred to as fitting him "when a boy." They continue to act as though money, not love, is the factor that will save us; as though economics, not humanitarian values, is the principle that should guide us; and as though short-term corporate profits, not the people of the United States, should be the primary beneficiary of their largess.

Such thinking is not the light that guides us; it is the darkness that blinds us.

In fact, in order to survive and thrive in the twenty-first century, we must make our love for one another the central factor in all political decision-making. In the words of Martin

Luther King Jr., "We must all learn to live together as brothers or we will all perish together as fools. . . . We are tied together in the single garment of destiny, caught in an inescapable network of mutuality." We heard those words in the twentieth century, but we need to hear them now in a whole new way. We can no longer afford to think of them as mere metaphor. They are directives that speak to the realities of our time. We need to recognize what they mean—not deny what they mean and simply hope that things work out.

We need to recognize that climate change poses an existential threat to our survival.

We need to recognize that the physical resources of the planet are not unlimited, and that in abusing them we are endangering ourselves and our children's children.

We need to recognize that the endless application of brute force will not bring peace to the world, and that only the soul force of justice, meaningful human relationships, forgiveness, and compassion can end the scourge of violence on our streets and throughout the world.

We need to recognize that to fail our children is to destroy our future.

A politics that fails to honor the knowing of the heart is a politics that fails the quintessential task of paving the way to a survivable future. Love, not money, should be our new bottom line.

# The Power Within Us

Today we are not in the middle of a covert corporate take-over of our democracy; we're in the middle of an overt corporate takeover of our democracy. An establishment that thinks traditional political strategizing alone can override this threat is not as sophisticated as it thinks it is. In fact, it is naive.

The forces of unbridled corporate power are hugely funded, politically savvy, and active on local, state, and federal levels. They don't care if we defeat their candidates in a particular election, because behind that candidate they have several more. They've shown they're not above suppressing votes, hacking machines (or conspiring with those who do), or spreading lies to the American people. Only a massive wave of conscious citizenship, alert to what is happening at every level of our government, can override their nefarious influence.

The conscious citizen is working on more cylinders than the traditional political activist. Not just the power of the intellect, but also the powers of imagination and love, are necessary to overcome the influence of the new aristocracy.

With our imagination, we give birth to new realities. We can envision the world we want and then work back from there. We can *imagine* a world at peace, a planet healed, and all sentient beings happy. We can visualize those things and commit ourselves to their manifestation.

When we do, we are confronted by the gap between what we are imagining and what we are currently creating. Is America's foreign policy a prescription for world peace? Are our environmental policies a prescription for a healed planet? Are our education and economic policies a prescription for economic growth for any but a few? No wonder so many people on the spiritual path avoid politics altogether. It's hard to meditate in the morning, then read the newspaper and see how billion-dollar American arms sales and technical support to Saudi Arabia are contributing to the starvation of tens of thousands in Yemen. It's even harder to see when our own leaders confound all efforts to stop the evil. It's hard to watch a beautiful sunset on a gorgeous beach and consider that millions of children in some other part of the country go to school each day in schools that don't even have needed supplies. The cognitive dissonance is painful.

Yet being with that dissonance is important; it is our soul work. The purpose of our lives is to close the gap between what could be and what too often is. Goodness must be willed; it doesn't necessarily happen of itself. It's not enough to not intend to do harm; our moral responsibility is to intend to do good. And then do it.

That is why it's our responsibility to protest when our nation, with our tax dollars and in our name, does wrong. If we're morally responsible for monitoring our own souls, then we're morally responsible, as well, for monitoring the soul of our nation.

It's not as though the majority of our citizens don't want a peaceful world; of course we do. The problem is that our political and economic systems are not currently placed at the service of that vision. If one's main goal is the attainment of power or the creation of short-term profit, then what is truly peace-creating, loving, behavior is often dropped by the wayside or given short shrift.

The things that in fact do the most to improve our democracy and create peace among us are not the things that make immediate money for our economic overlords. Do we truly want world peace? Then expanding economic opportunities for women and educational opportunities for children, not just profits for military manufacturers, should be at the core of our national security agenda. Do we really want a healthy environment? Then we must stop using the Environmental Protection Agency to shore up profits for fossil fuel companies at the expense of their effect on climate change. Do we really want a long-term healthy economy? Then we should massively realign our investments in the direction of support for health, education, and culture among America's children.

Old systems do not die willingly, particularly when they control gargantuan amounts of wealth and power. From the dismantling of environmental protections to economic policies that increase the gaps between rich and poor to the destruction of indigenous wisdom and peoples in the name of economic "progress" to the often unthinking extension of our military prowess, we have been moving away from, not toward, the realization of humanity's highest hopes for life on earth.

Yet we would do well to remember the laws of evolution. Any species behaving in maladaptive ways will either evolve or become extinct. A world in which we habitually and powerfully attack not only each other but even our own habitat, is a world the laws of evolution will not support.

Our species will either evolve to a more heart-centered consciousness, choosing a greater reverence for planet and people, or we will go extinct due to collective behavior that is maladaptive for our survival. No change in government will fundamentally save us unless we are willing to evolve as a species from one with prodigious intellect and technological power but disconnected from its heart to one that puts reverence and devotion and love before all else. As with any other species, our opportunity for survival lies in the presence of an evolutionary alternative, or mutation. For the human species, that mutation is a mutation of consciousness. It is represented by the great spiritual masters who have lived among us, teaching the message of compassion and love. Only a spiritual leap forward will save us from the evils of the world.

The weight of history is on our shoulders now. This year—not next year or the year after that—we are called upon to put aside unimportant things and get to the work of correcting our evolutionary course.

# 3

# LOVE AND CONFLICT
## DISAGREEING WITH LOVE

After giving an Easter sermon at a Unity church in Raleigh, North Carolina, I went for Mexican food with four of the church's congregants. With me sat two ministers, plus the husband of one and the son of the other. I was happy to be sharing margaritas and conversation with lovely people on a beautiful Easter day. Then, after some pleasant chitchat about spirituality, children, and relationships, I ventured into tougher territory.

"So," I said, "I want to talk about politics."

A moment of silence. My friends looked at me intently. They had heard me talk about politics the night before (feedback: "I don't agree with a lot of what you say about politics"), then forgiveness and Jesus that morning (feedback: "I love it when you talk about God").

"Did you vote for Trump?" I asked the minister's husband.

"Yes, I did," he replied.

"Did you?" I asked his wife.

"I didn't vote," she said. "I couldn't vote for either one."

"Did you?" I asked the minister sitting next to me.

"I did."

I knew that the minister's son had voted for Donald Trump, because in the car on the way to the church he had explained to me his conservative politics.

I looked at all of them and, after a couple of moments, said simply, "Can you please tell me what it is I'm not seeing?"

They then proceeded to tell me a variation of something I'd heard before: that they didn't particularly care for the president as a man, but they liked what he was doing for America. Where I saw an attack on the press, they saw "standing up to fake news"; where I saw the dismantling of environmental protections, they saw "needed deregulation"; where I saw the words of an authoritarian dictator, they saw a man who "doesn't really mean those things."

A politics of love has as much to do with how we listen as with the things we say. Partly because I had shared with them an Easter service filled with prayer and meditation that morning, and partly because my friends are lovely people whom I genuinely like, I could hear them at lunch that day without reactivity. I felt no constriction in my heart, no negativity, no judgment.

We were meeting in Rumi's field "beyond good and bad, right and wrong," which is the only place where souls *can* meet.

I heard a thing or two that deepened my understanding of where they were coming from, and I like to think that maybe I said a thing or two that had an impact on them as well. I mentioned at the table that it should be part of our spiritual practice to remember that no one has a monopoly on truth. Our capacity to listen to each other is more urgently needed now than our capacity to yell at each other. Hate anywhere is a toxin everywhere, and if we demonize each other personally, then we're wrong even if we're right.

It's my personal goal—at times I'm successful and at times I'm not—to dissolve the personal negativity I sometimes feel toward those with whom I politically disagree, while retaining the passion and conviction of my disagreement. I've read enough words of Mahatma Gandhi and Martin Luther King Jr. and studied enough treatises on political nonviolence to know the goal. I know that we have to *be* the change. It's practicing all that that's sometimes hard.

All of us have our fingers pointing at someone today. "They're the problem." "No, *they're* the problem." But in a spiritual sense, the pointed finger is the problem.

The answer isn't what you think or what I think; the Answer, with a capital "A," is a place in consciousness where no one is demonized and everyone is appreciated for the innocence at their core. That's the only place where we can all be heard, and heard without judgment. Not enough of us today feel from others—or grant to others—the emotional permission to express our views or theirs without ridicule or dishonor. We've become a nation of bad listeners, concerned more with getting our point across than with hearing what someone else is trying to say.

Many years ago, I was visiting then-congressman Dennis Kucinich, a progressive Democrat, at the US Capitol in Washington, DC; at the time, the country was convulsed by the impeachment proceedings against President Bill Clinton. As we entered an elevator Lindsey Graham, then a conservative Republican congressman (now a senator), came out of the elevator, and the two men greeted each other affectionately. After the elevator door closed, I made a disapproving comment about Congressman Graham.

Dennis looked at me like I was nuts. "What are you *talking* about?" he said. "He's a great guy!"

I'd heard Graham on television railing against President Clinton, and I had made judgments based on that. I mentioned a particular TV show in which I'd seen conservatives doing political "crossfire" with liberals, and I was decidedly in one camp.

"That's just TV, Marianne!" said Dennis. "It has nothing to do with how things work around here. Lindsey is a great guy, and we work together on a lot of things."

Now my blood was boiling again, not at conservative politicians but at what had happened to our public sphere: we had turned our politics into a boxing match, what should be high-minded debate into a psychological blood sport, and it was already doing damage.

I was right to be concerned. Decades later, entire generations have grown up thinking that this is what politics is—a boxing match and a blood sport. Until we address that issue and deal with it, we will continue to spiral into an even darker night of the American soul. How we are talking to each other is as corrupt and corrupting as what anyone is saying.

# Just Say No to Contempt

Some people argue that since it's so hard to have a political conversation these days without getting into some kind of negativity, we should simply avoid the subject of politics altogether.

I disagree.

Avoiding political discussion is what got us into this mess. We need to transform our political conversations, not suppress them. Disagreeing with someone doesn't mean we're "attacking" them. Standing up to evil doesn't mean we're being "judgmental." And there's nothing holy about using spirituality as a justification for political disengagement. "Spiritual" people *should* be having the difficult conversations. We should be the biggest grown-ups in the room.

At Easter lunch that day, I mentioned my concern about a pattern of unarmed black men being shot by police. To me, this should not be a conservative issue or a progressive issue. Who among us *wouldn't* be horrified when a young man, father of two, standing in his grandmother's backyard with nothing in his hands or on his person but a cell phone, is shot in the back twenty times by police who'd been called to check out a report of vandalism in the neighborhood?

One of my new friends told me that he couldn't join me in

my concern because he "supports law enforcement." At which point, I said it was insulting to suggest that those who have a problem with that shooting do *not* support law enforcement!

"But murder is murder," I exclaimed, "no matter who is doing it!"

His mother then said that she'd had a problem with the statement in my talk the night before that a country in which police can just kill people at will is called a police state.

"But it *is!*" I told her.

It doesn't show lack of support for law enforcement to point out that only in a police state can police kill whomever they want, at will. That might not be a fear that I or any of my white friends live with on a daily basis, but there are people of color who do. That is simply a fact. Does it mean that I love America any less, or support law enforcement any less, that this disturbs me greatly?

I believe that the vast majority of police officers in America are good people who take extraordinary risks to ensure the safety of the rest of us every day. I am deeply grateful for that, as we all should be. But most doctors, most lawyers, and most teachers are good people too. That doesn't mean that all of them are, or that those who aren't should not be held accountable.

I can't see how anyone can defend what they consider "American values" with a defense of attitudes that undermine those values. On the other hand, I know I'm spiritually off-base myself if I close my heart to someone because of my perception that they're closing theirs. Who among us hasn't found ourselves at times judging people for "being judgmental"? Ah, the irony. From a spiritual perspective, if someone is driving us crazy, then the deeper issue is still our own craziness. The work is always on ourselves.

While the ego always monitors other people's thoughts and behavior, the spirit would have us monitor only our own. And since everyone can subconsciously register where we're coming from, regardless of what we say, it's only in purifying our own hearts that we have any chance of touching someone else's. In the words of Martin Luther King Jr., "We have little morally persuasive power with someone who can feel our underlying contempt."

That has to be our goal now: not mere defeat of political opponents, but also engagement in the art of moral persuasion—the ability to so commune with the heart of another that real communication can occur.

I don't think it was an accident that the conversation with my Trump-supporting friends that day took place on Easter Sunday—not for symbolic reasons, but for literal ones. We had spent time together thinking about the infinite power of love that morning. We had prayed and meditated together. It was Easter, for goodness' sake! We were *predisposed* to loving each other, and that made all the difference. There was no way I could see them as stereotypes, and I assume that they could not see me that way either. My friends and I were able to honor each other, even while we disagreed, and engage on serious political issues without compromising our convictions.

Our political as well as our personal salvation is indeed a revolution of the heart. I knew that at the deepest level my differences with my friends were semantic. All of us agreed on basic values; we were simply worlds apart on what those values looked like when expressed in political terms.

Gandhi said that "politics should be sacred." By that, he didn't mean religious; he meant that the level of our political conversation should be sacred. It should be the level of conversation we have in therapy, or support groups, or intimate conversation. The level from which we speak determines the level of our understanding.

The sacred place within us lies beyond such polarity as liberal and conservative. In the words of Dwight Eisenhower, "The American mind at its best is both liberal and conservative." High-minded conservative principles and high-minded liberal ones form a creative synergy, a yin and yang of American politics. Both are great American political traditions, and both support the ideals of democracy. The threat to our democracy comes from neither of those traditions. The threat is authoritarian corporatism, which does not respect serious conservatism, serious progressivism, universal humanitarian values, or even democracy itself.

We *need* to be able to discuss these things. Whenever anyone says, "We're not going to talk about politics or religion," I'm so like, "Well, that leaves me out at dinner!" Our tendency these days to have a political conversation only with people who already agree with us—exacerbated by all the mean-spiritedness on social media—is destructive to the social fabric of our country. It is intellectually lazy to stereotype someone just because they see things differently, and it lacks emotional discipline to lash out at people for the simple fact that they disagree with you.

It is essential to nonviolent communication that we affirm the dignity and goodness of other people, even if we disagree with them. That is the sweet spot underlying honorable debate: to first assume someone's basic innocence and speak to them from there. The ego's temptation is always to attack, to create separation, to make another person wrong—especially when we're so sure we're right! As someone who can jump into snark or sarcasm more easily than I should, I know the dead end those attitudes represent. Making another person feel guilty will never build unity or goodwill; only blessing, not blaming, can do that. All judgment does is to shut people down emotionally and psychologically.

I was struck by a tweet I saw once: someone said that her grandmother had told her: "Just remember that when the two of you are fighting, it's you two versus the fighting, not you versus him." That struck me, because who among us has not at times given in to the temptation to demonize those with whom we disagree?

Only in a totalitarian society is everyone supposed to toe the line and see things the same way. No one owes it to us to agree with us about anything, including politics. No side of the political spectrum has a monopoly on righteousness or values, and anyone who argues otherwise represents a viewpoint unworthy of who we are.

# Fight the Fighting

n 2002, I was invited by Coretta Scott King to speak at the Ebenezer Baptist Church in Atlanta at the birthday celebration for Dr. King. It was a great honor to be invited, and I was prepared to give a speech about the differences between Dr. King's philosophy of nonviolence and President George W. Bush's statements after 9/11.

Having arrived at the church, I was escorted to a room where I was to wait before meeting Mrs. King. When the greeter came in and asked, "Are you ready to meet Mrs. King and Mrs. Bush now?" I was stunned. I had had no idea that Laura Bush was going to be there. I was totally unprepared.

*Okay, Ms. Nonviolent Feminist, how are you are going to pull this off, talking about the president right in front of the woman who is married to him?*

I had to think quickly, which was probably a good thing. I prayed for both women, and for myself, and then I had to go on to the pulpit. The only way I could think of to handle the situation was to turn around to Mrs. Bush every time I spoke of the president and say, "Mrs. Bush, we're praying for your husband at this difficult time." And then, as respectfully as I could, I'd let it rip.

At the end of my talk, I went to shake hands first with Mrs.

King and then with Mrs. Bush. When I put my hand out to Laura, I started to apologize if I had offended her. But she graciously put her finger to my lips and, nodding her head, said, "Shhh! You did *good*!" I knew in that moment that she realized what had happened. She knew where she was going that day; she realized that I disagreed with her husband, but that I had made every effort to do so with respect. She affirmed me for that, and for her kind behavior toward me that day she earned my respect as well.

My standing with those two women in that moment is a memory that is frozen in my brain. In many ways, we couldn't have been more different, yet in that moment we couldn't have been more the same. In our own way, we were experiencing politics as sacred.

We don't all have to agree with each other, but *how* we disagree is a crucial issue in a politics of love. I've learned the hard way in my life that the inappropriate indulgence of anger is a form of self-sabotage. We're not only responsible for our thoughts; we're also responsible for our behavior. And our behavior includes not only what we say but how we say it.

I notice on my social media that there are two different types of critics: those who disagree with me with reason and respect, and those who attack and insult me personally. From the first, I can learn things I hadn't thought about or known before; I can appreciate what they bring to my awareness. From the latter, however, I feel the energy of attack and then feel my heart constrict in response.

Nonviolence means more than giving up physical violence; it means giving up emotional and psychological violence as well. Whether we attack a person physically or not, an attack is still an attack. Every thought we think takes form on some level, then boomerangs back to us after we put it out there. So many mental missiles are flying through the air today, you can almost feel a new American Civil War raging on invisible planes.

This is not a time for knee-jerk attacks on people who don't agree with us, although it's absolutely a time to stand passionately for the things we believe in. That balance is challenging at times, but we owe it to ourselves, and to our country, to arrive at the place where we can bless even those with whom we disagree politically.

Since President Trump's 2016 election, such efforts have been more challenging than ever. Not every situation is like my lunch in North Carolina, where we had to hold on to nonjudgment for only as long as it took us to share a meal! Some of us have close friends or family who vehemently disagree with us politically these days. And in some situations, those disagreements are tearing us apart.

For instance, two of my close girlfriends are enthusiastic Trump supporters and I am not. In both cases, we found early on that not discussing politics was probably the best way to go. But my friend Alana and I have tried to find a way past that: to communicate in a way where we can both be true to our politics, yet true to the bonds of our affection for each other as well. Sometimes we succeed, and sometimes we don't.

During the year after Trump's 2016 election, Alana asked me if I would help promote her skin care line on my social media. I didn't see skin care promotion as appropriate for either my Facebook or Twitter pages, but I wanted to be a supportive friend. I settled on an idea for Instagram; I wrote what I thought was a cute little caption under the picture of her holding her skin care product, saying that we didn't agree on politics, but hey, who doesn't agree about collagen! I thought it was harmless, fun, and even demonstrative of how those of us who disagree politically can make it through these times with our personal relationships intact.

Several people who posted seemed to agree and appreciated our efforts to protect our friendship. Yet many did not. Some of those who did not, in fact, were vicious. They would no longer follow me if I was even friends with a Trump supporter! The ridiculous assumptions about who I am, and even more so the outrageous assumptions about who Alana is, were so devoid of anything approaching dignified disagreement that I ended up deleting the entire post.

None of us, no matter what our politics, are invulnerable to the machinations of the negative ego. A smug, self-righteous, intolerant left-winger poses no less danger to the emotional fabric of this nation than a smug, self-righteous, intolerant right-winger. Something I need to tell myself constantly these days is that not every comment needs a follow-up opinion! My mother used to say, "Count to ten before you speak." Sometimes I need to count to fifteen.

As an author, I notice that if I write something in a book that a reader doesn't like, I'll probably never know about it. It's sort of none of my business. Maybe that person will stop reading the book or even give it a harsh review somewhere. But with social media, everyone now has a public platform from which to espouse their opinions immediately—and boy, do they!

It's as though no one today has any impulse control; anger and anxiety spew out everywhere, making much of our public discourse dangerously toxic and mean-spirited. From both Left and the Right come harmful shutdowns, aimed at those whose only transgression was the audacity to share an opinion that doesn't align with someone else's preconceived notion of truth. Adding to the chaos, a constant bombardment of disconcerting news has millions of Americans on edge each day. Our very nervous systems are assaulted by these things, increasing the possibility of mistakes and inappropriate responses. And all of it mitigates against the wise, deep thinking and communication so needed among us now.

Our tendency to fly off the handle politically can be a challenge for all of us. A politics of love speaks to more than our political opinions; it speaks to the quality of our personhood, our emotional self-discipline, and our ability to embody the love and peace that we claim we so want for the world.

For that, there is no greater ameliorative than prayer and meditation. Aligning our nervous systems with the highest frequency of heart and mind is a prerequisite for enduring and transforming the times in which we live. In the words of His Holiness the Dalai Lama, "In order to save the world, we must have a plan. But no plan will work unless we meditate." You can't be a light of the world and a nervous wreck at the same time.

At times like these, we *should* stand up, we *should* express ourselves, and we *should* rise up to protect our democracy. But we need to do so without lowering our personal energy to the level of those who would seek to destroy it. Michelle Obama said the words we all need to remember, in our personal interactions as well as in our politics: "When they go low, we go high."

For women—and for any formerly disempowered group not allowed to say much for several centuries—it can be hard to know how to talk at first. It's like the dirty water that spurts out of a bathtub that hasn't been used for a while; you just have to let it do its thing for a bit, and then clear water will begin to flow. During that time, however, we can too easily swing between two dysfunctional poles: either we swallow our truth, or blurt it out too harshly.

But angry communication is a self-sabotaging trap. The word *communication* has the word *commune* inside it, reminding us that when we speak without love, we're rarely communicating in a way that will be heard. The ego can be so sly, making us feel we're "communicating" something when what we're actually doing is blocking communication entirely.

The fact that I spoke doesn't necessarily mean that you heard me. To genuinely communicate, I need to be responsible not only for what I say but for creating the heart space between us that enables you to hear it. When people feel judged and attacked, they shut down and do not hear us.

"I was just communicating my feelings!" you might say. But being "authentic" isn't necessarily so great when we're authentically angry. Real authenticity is more than emotional self-indulgence. It takes inner work to surrender our fear and retrieve our love, remembering that the person we're speaking to is an innocent child of God no less than we are, and *then* choosing to speak. A politics of love involves taking personal responsibility as much for *how* we do something as for *what* we do, and even for who we are while we're doing it.

Today, things are moving so quickly that we often text or speak or do whatever we do before remembering to surrender our anger to God. That prayer of surrender matters, because it literally changes our nervous system. It realigns our thought processes and our emotions. This kind of practice is particularly important today, when many have learned the hard way that there's no way to delete a tweet. In the last few years, major careers have been ruined for no less.

Emotions are running high, and personal self-discipline is hugely important. Through prayer, meditation, and forgiveness, the serious spiritual activist accepts the responsibility of holding to our love despite the temptation to disavow it. In order to transform the chaos in the world, we must address the chaos in ourselves.

About a year ago, I moved into an apartment in New York City. Having moved there from a building that had a beautiful, peaceful view of a church courtyard, I was worried that I wouldn't be able to find such peace and tranquility on a busy midtown street. After being in my new apartment for a day, I was gazing at the view outside and realized I was offered here another kind of peace: the spiritual opportunity to bless all the people in the buildings I could see from my window. After several minutes of thinking about how wonderful all that was—about all the people working and living in those buildings to whom I could send my love on any given day—I realized that I was looking straight at Trump Tower from my window!

You don't have to be an enlightened master to appreciate how perfect that is. *Great, Marianne,* I said to myself. *This is perfect. Every time you walk through the apartment you can bless him in your mind and feel blessed, or you can attack him in your mind and feel attacked.*

Spiritual law is unalterable: if we focus on the guilt in others, we'll see guilt in ourselves; if we focus on the innocence in others, we'll feel the innocence within ourselves. Perception is a choice.

I have chosen to bless the president, not only for his sake but for my own peace of mind. I pray for his happiness and for his enlightenment. But that doesn't mean I have to agree with him. And it doesn't mean I won't do anything possible to resist his policies when they're counter to the values of our democracy or work hard to defeat him at the polls in 2020.

A politics of love is not naive. It is strategic. It is the only power that can override hate. No amount of intellectual analysis or traditional political strategy can override the dangerous energies unleashed by cultlike political forces. Cultlike figures appeal to something beyond the rational brain; in fact, the danger they present is that they can *override* the rational brain. And we must override *that*.

When lies are systematically presented as truth in order to obfuscate the truth, and are done so specifically for political purposes, we have a serious problem on our hands. Neither intellectual analysis nor political strategy nor brute force alone can annihilate the explosive energies of politicized hatred. Only a higher truth can prevail against that which would obliterate truth entirely. Only the power of the heart can triumph over manipulations of the mind. Only the power of the soul can override the mortal dangers posed by soullessness in our politics or anywhere else.

# Land of the Free, Home of the Brave

Many claim today that they've been "traumatized" by Trump's presidency; I've even seen articles written by psychotherapists who call such trauma a syndrome! But this is not the time to coddle our preciousness. Surely those who walked across the bridge at Selma, Alabama, on Bloody Sunday 1965 were traumatized, not knowing whether at any time the dogs or the hoses, or even bullets, would be used against them. Yet they walked. And anxiety? Surely the suffragettes who were thrown into prison and force-fed through feeding tubes suffered from anxiety. Yes, we feel wounded, and that's because the times in which we live are wounding. But who have we become that we're so enamored with our woundedness? None of us has time to finish our trauma work before rising to the defense of our country.

This is not a time for personal weakness, but for strength. The only real strength is love; love makes us vulnerable, but in a way that makes us strong. It doesn't turn us into wounded birds. It makes us powerful and strong and courageous, intellectually and emotionally.

We must not indulge our hopelessness now, resigning ourselves to the idea that the concentrated assaults on everything from the planet to our democracy have succeeded to such a degree that it's no longer possible to stop them. A miracle is a shift in our thinking from fear to love, and when our thinking shifts, then everything changes. Synapses in the brain, relationship vectors between and among us, new possibilities both psychological and material, automatically unfold. Things are hopeless only if miracles do not occur, and because miracles *do* occur naturally as expressions of love, things are not actually hopeless.

Surely the abolition of slavery at one time seemed like a hopeless cause. Surely women's suffrage at one time seemed like a hopeless cause. Surely ending racial segregation at one time seemed like a hopeless cause. Hope springs eternal because life springs eternal, and life springs eternal with infinite possibility.

America is down, but not for the count. A new democratic revolution has already begun in the hearts and minds of millions. A powerful resistance movement is making itself felt, and it will not be stopped. People are realizing that democracy is not just a right but a responsibility, a gift we were given that matters to more than just us. It matters to the ages, and that is why we will do whatever it takes to make sure that it survives.

Human beings are the authors of our history. It is a story that we write and have the power to rewrite. For a nation as well as for an individual, the universe is merciful when we take responsibility for our mistakes and do what is necessary to correct them.

America was a country that had everything, was given everything, was blessed beyond comprehension, yet chose to sell its soul to the highest bidder. We put economics before love, sales before ethics, and our government on the bidding block. We have treated the earth with lack of reverence, democracy as though we could take it for granted, and justice as relevant only to ourselves. Too often, and in too many different ways, we allowed the values and principles that made our nation great to fall by the wayside, as though they mattered not.

We wrote that story ourselves—we need to admit that—and now we can write another one. Atoning for and making amends for our errors, we are released from their consequences. Where we have strayed off course we can return to the path of righteousness. What we have forgotten we can remember, and when we have fallen we can rise back up.

No conscious person can sit out the current crisis. Crises are never convenient, but they happen. They demand our attention, and our excellence, often when we are most afraid. But we must be brave now, for it's not just our democracy that's at risk. The sacrifice of our values, both personal and political, has put *everything* at risk.

Our challenge is to rise to the divine within us, casting out the shadows of our own lower nature. We must do this not only as individuals but as members of a larger society. It might be in our lower nature to fight, but it is in our higher nature to love. It might be in our lower nature to exploit the earth for our own purposes, but it is in our higher nature to be good and reverent stewards of the earth. Humanity stands at a crossroads now: will we serve only the dictates of our material selves, or will we rise to the full embrace of our spiritual selves? There will be consequences either way.

A world unaligned with the ways of our spiritual nature has begun to fall apart because *anything* unaligned with the ways of our higher nature inevitably falls apart. The mind unaligned with love becomes aligned with fear, and fear now threatens to overtake our planet. We are challenged to regain spiritual balance, both in ourselves and in our world.

To do so is our purpose on earth, and it is our only sustainable option.

# Loving Hearts, Passionate Action

Several years ago, I read a wonderful novel by Sue Monk Kidd titled *The Invention of Wings*. The book is about two historical figures during the nineteenth century named Sarah and Angelina Grimke. The Grimke sisters were born into a slave-owning family in South Carolina, then later became converted by Quakers to the abolitionist cause.

Reading Kidd's book made me think about what it meant for someone raised in a slave-owning environment to awaken to the evils of slavery. This spiritual awakening is encapsulated in a lyric from "Amazing Grace": "I . . . was blind but now I see."

The Grimke sisters took a huge personal journey that is relevant to our own day. Being antislavery in nineteenth-century America would have meant not agreeing with slavery, with practicing it oneself. It might have meant not living in a slave-owning state. But being antislavery, in and of itself, did not necessarily move the needle for one slave. A huge internal bridge was crossed—psychologically, emotionally, and spiritually—when one went from being antislavery to being an abolitionist. It meant going from "I don't agree with it" to "*Not on my watch.*"

A politics of love, then, takes a stand. False positivism has no place in our personal lives or in our political lives either. There are certain issues that call upon us to be as passionate with our no as with our yes. When money and not love is our bottom line—when we place economics before our humanitarian values—then unnecessary harm inevitably results. People suffer, children die, and the earth is damaged. Once you see that connection, you cannot unsee it. In the words of Elie Wiesel, "We must take sides. Neutrality helps the oppressor, never the victim. Silence encourages the tormentor, never the tormented."

We do not transcend darkness by simply ignoring it. There is a difference between transcendence and denial. We deny evil its power not by denying its existence, but by denying it room to fester in the sinews of our hearts and minds.

Some people say we shouldn't focus on our political problems, because what we focus on expands. But that's as ridiculous as an oncologist saying, "It's cancer, but only stage 1, so let's not think about it." Some negative things expand for the very reason that we did *not* look at them.

There's nothing negative about naming things that need to be named. There's nothing negative about yelling "Fire!" when in fact the house is burning down. And there's nothing that we cannot do when the heart is filled with love.

# 4

# AN ECONOMICS OF LOVE

## A NEW BOTTOM LINE

The Latin root of the word *economy* refers to the management of a household. There is no better example of right management of a household than the economy of nature. It is a perfect ecosystem in which nothing is wasted, every part of the whole has a perfect relationship to every other part, and all things inherently move in the direction of greater life.

The problem with modern economics is that it does not honor the economy of nature, but rather has set itself up in competition with nature. It is based on the organization of goods and services for the goal of profit, rather than for the goal of furthering life. As such is out of alignment with the enlightened thinking necessary to guide us to a sustainable future.

When viewed through the lens of modern economics, the primary driver of the economy is profit. When viewed through the lens of an enlightened economics for the twenty-first century, the primary mover of the economy is human creativity.

When financialization replaces production as the dominant way to make money—as has happened over the last four decades in America—the dignity and creativity of human beings is sacrificed. For example, when capitalists take over a profitable company that produces and sells goods, carve it into pieces, shut down operations, put people out of work, and bankrupt the company, but then *they* make millions of dollars doing it. That is the kind of scenario that has resulted from the separation of capitalism from ethics. It is unconscious capitalism and an amoral economics. Human beings are there simply to serve the economy, when in fact the economy should be there to serve human beings. Transaction replaces relationship as the main mode of human organization. And all hell breaks loose from there.

Enlightened economics is moral, in that it honors the needs of people and planet before the needs of the marketplace. Interestingly, Adam Smith, the primary analyst of modern capitalism, argued that the free market cannot exist outside an ethical context. Yet today it does, which means that it is not free. Since the 1980s, economic policy in the United States has been driven by a decidedly amoral perspective positing that the demands of the marketplace—unlimited by any ethical restraint—should be our financial bottom line.

A healthy, free economy is about more than numbers. It is about more than things. It is about more than goods. *It is about us.*

An unconscious capitalism—freed from government protection of workers and the environment through the removal of Glass-Steagall legislation, global trade deals that fail to protect the American worker, taxes favoring wealthy corporations, union busting, and more—has done incalculable harm to democracy, people, and planet. In the United States, it has destroyed our middle class and turned the majority of our citizens into little more than serfs to a system over which they feel they have no control. It has made the short-term profit maximization of multinational corporations our society's bottom line, claiming this would lift all boats when in fact it has left millions without even a life vest. It has made people subservant to things, and loving human relationships secondary to money. It has replaced the tyranny of a king with the tyranny of an amoral economic system.

And it is time for this to change. The harm it is doing to our society is more than political or economic. It is a moral rot that leads to political corruption that leads to human devastation.

While it's the task of economic policy to promote prosperity, more than money is needed to make life prosperous. True prosperity includes a sense of security and well-being that goes beyond finances. The ultimate prosperity is dwelling in the sense that all things are possible. And the ultimate American Dream is the establishment of a society in which, if anyone works hard enough, then they have a reason to feel that way.

Our economics should honor that dream, not function in a way that as often as not shatters it. To survive, people need our base-level physical needs met. But to thrive, people need more than that. We need meaning. We need spiritual sustenance. We need a sense that our lives matter.

Our economic system should serve, not stymie, a genuine prosperity. It should free, not limit, the ability of all citizens to harness their creativity in service of something larger than themselves. That lifts people to our higher place, out of which creativity and energy flow naturally.

That is why education, health, infrastructure, and culture should come first, for they are the most serious investments a society can make in the happiness and well-being of its people. Happy, secure people are much more likely to produce creativity and wealth than are those who are struggling just to survive.

We should not just ask if the economy is healthy; we should ask if *we* are healthy, in every way that the word has significance. When we are healthy, our economy is more likely to be as well.

Our political establishment posits the idea that a healthy economy guarantees a happy society. If that were true, given that we are the richest nation on earth, we should be the happiest. Yet clearly we are not. High rates of depression, suicide, economic anxiety, drug addiction, incarceration, and environmental toxicity are not the marks of happiness.

A healthy economy is currently defined as total output of gross domestic product (GDP). But GDP should not be seen as an accurate measure of our well-being, whether economically or in any other way. It overlooks the issues of working conditions, environmental well-being, and health and safety, among other things. It doesn't take into account the chronic anxiety, opioid addiction, and emotional state of millions of Americans traumatized simply by living in their neighborhoods.

Our primary economic indicators measure products but don't measure us. In that sense, our view of economics is unnatural; it is an idolatrous way of thinking that bows more to material values than to universal human values. When we turn our focus toward being a good society rather than a rich society, a lot more people will be richer in every way.

What is referred to as an economy that's "doing well" is actually one in which, however low the official unemployment rate may be, 40 percent of all Americans struggle to make ends meet and have a hard time covering their food, shelter, transportation, and health care costs. Many of them are referred to as the "working poor." Yes, they are working. But they are not doing well. Many official figures coming out of Washington do not reflect their difficulties so much as make a mockery of them. Our government's attitude toward economic despair is often less about ameliorating it and more about announcing to the desperate that they're not really desperate.

An economics of love makes people, not products, the focus of our investments. An economics of love does not take an unsophisticated view of finance, but in fact has a more sophisticated view of how money is created. Our greatest creative energy comes not from outside us but from inside us; therefore, anything that supports our internal growth supports our capacity to economically thrive. It's long been recognized that ensuring that people feel respected for their contribution to a workplace and valued for who they are as people does more to increase their productivity than does money alone.

Money is created by creativity, not the other way around. The source of our creativity is within. It is part of who we are. The greatest proof of this is evident in any kindergarten anywhere in the world.

Consider, for instance, a Montessori classroom, where children are allowed to roam among play and work stations. Are they not industrious? Are they not creative? Are they not in their own way entrepreneurial? Most of our economic theories were invented by men who had not spent a particularly great amount of time around small children—not even their own. If they had, perhaps they would have realized that people are naturally creative and industrious, *particularly in the first eight years of life.*

An economics in sync with the more enlightened thinking of the twenty-first century is an economics based on two main factors: one, feed the creativity of the child in order to foster the productivity of the adult that child will become; and two, remove as much unnecessary anxiety as possible from people in order to unleash their creativity and productivity.

It is not as though children want to create, but then lose the desire as they grow older. Rather, creativity is too often beaten out of people. What happens in a society like ours is that so many people live with daily economic stress and anxiety that their creative juices are sapped. (*What will happen if I lose my job and I don't have benefits? What will happen if I get sick? What will happen if one of my kids gets sick? How will I pay for my kids to go to college? How will I pay off my college loans? Will I have enough money to retire without going broke?*) Some argue that we "can't afford" programs such as universal health care and the cancellation of college loan debt, yet the sleight of hand there is preposterous. Every dollar invested in education is an investment in tomorrow's economy. Every dollar invested in people is an investment in their productivity, and thus a larger consumer base. Our current economic functioning has nothing to do with long-term economic planning, and everything to do with leeching from our system every possible short-term advantage for a minority of our citizens. Thus, we steal from our children, our planet, and our future. If we were really thinking about our long-term economic good, we would be massively realigning our investments not toward our economic overlords, but toward we the people of the United States.

Americans of every age are entrepreneurial by temperament, and when we're supported in such endeavors and allowed to thrive, we are naturally productive. Each of us carries within us greater God-given potential than most of us will ever actualize. That is as true of a poor person as it is of a rich person. No socioeconomic group has a monopoly on the desire to create, to contribute, and to do so with dignity. Millions of Americans work hard and are deeply creative, yet can hardly make ends meet. That doesn't mean they're any more "lazy" than rich people. The often articulated correlation between wealth-creation and willingness to work—and the concomitant correlation between poverty and unwillingness to work—is false. In fact, millions of America's most industrious citizens—people who get up before dawn each day, raise families, and work the hardest—struggle daily to make ends meet.

Such assumptions as those mentioned above are simply vicious stereotypes used to justify the leeching of resources from those who need it most. The majority of America's poor are not looking for handouts but for a fair shot—which too often they are not receiving now. There is a difference between handouts and simple economic justice. In the words of Martin Luther King Jr., "When they give it to the rich, they call it a subsidy; when they give it to the poor, they call it a handout." Governmental policy skewed in the direction of giving more to those who already have more, and less to those who already have less, is neither just nor democratic.

We defer to the needs of the market when instead we should be deferring to the needs of the people.

In the era of corporate conglomerates, employment has become nothing more than an amoral numbers game that is divorced from ethical considerations and turns the majority of people in the world into its servants. And too many people are left out of the game entirely, regardless of whether or not they have jobs. Financial figures are frequently used to obscure human realities that tell a different story than they do.

Traumatized, stressed-out, and unduly anxious people have a difficult time accessing their potential. Yes, some stress is healthy, but the economic stress of way too many Americans today is not that. Rather, these Americans endure the stress of having been cast out of nature's economy. For while nature has a way of supporting the living creatures within it, an economic system untethered to an ethical center has a way of casting out anyone and anything that does not serve it.

People want to feel that their work in the world expresses their creativity and life force and produces more than money—that it also produces dignity, self-satisfaction, and a sense of meaning and purpose in the world. An economics that offers nothing more than "employment," with little concern for what that employment offers above a baseline salary, is an economic model inadequate to the human demands of the twenty-first century—especially when that baseline salary is often not enough to enable hardworking people to support a family.

It is true—and to be respected—that successful businesses create jobs. But they are not the only engines of prosperity. And in truth, small businesses employ almost as many workers as big business does. It is only because big corporations have so much more money and influence over our government that they can skew economic policy in their favor. Making the profitability of large corporations the center of American economic policy has very little to do with actually serving the people, and everything to do with serving a donor class/economic ruling class that loves to present itself as America's great economic benefactor.

Business is important, and successful businesses are essential to a healthy economy. But the business sector is no more important or more essential to our economic good than education, health care, or any other avenue by which people are aided in their ability to self-actualize. Education, not big business, is the biggest job-creating sector. The greatest job-creator in America is not the businessperson but the teacher—one who doesn't simply give you a job, but prepares you for a career by providing you with the internal and external tools to create it. It is not just overseas outsourcing that has taken our jobs away; it is in equal measure our failure as a society to provide for the preparation of our citizens, from the earliest age, for the challenges of living in the twenty-first century.

Education, both intellectual and spiritual, is our largest engine of prosperity. Whole-person education prepares us to succeed. It gives us the training, hones the critical thought processes, and cultivates the attitudes that are essential to success. It gives people more than a path to a better job; it gives them a path to power. Perhaps that is what some American elites do not wish to see happen.

Health care is an engine of prosperity as well: first, because healthier people obviously have more energy; and second, because health insurance coverage takes away much of the economic anxiety that keeps people from soaring at full wingspan. Illness is one of the most common reasons people go bankrupt in this country: in the absence of health care coverage, illness robs us of both work and savings. It's hard to imagine how much more money would be circulating through the American economy if so many Americans weren't weighed down by illnesses—not only those they have but those they're terrified of getting.

Art and culture are engines of prosperity because they expand who we are as people and broaden the scope of our creativity. They energize us and deepen our humanity. Numerous studies have established that participation in the arts increases cognitive skills, yet more and more American children lack exposure to them in any meaningful way. In the richest country in the world, we have seen arts curricula fading fast from many of our schools, leaving only a market-based entertainment industry to take up the slack. A lot of good comes out of Hollywood—in movies, TV series, and internet productions—but artistic tastes that require cultivation, such as classical art and music and theater, should be taught in our schools as a means of basic cultural literacy.

By not vigorously supporting the arts, not providing universal health care, and undereducating so many of our citizens, today's economic system does more than keep money in the hands of a few—it keeps power in the hands of a few. It stymies genuine prosperity even while it claims to foster it.

None of us should accept the assumption that the business sector is the primary generator of prosperity. Such an assumption serves no one but the business sector, which then claims the right to undue economic advantages under the pretense that such advantages for the business sector foster a healthier economy.

Our esteemed economic councils shouldn't have just financiers in business suits serving on them; they should include schoolteachers and child psychologists, experts in liberal arts and technical education, and those who know best how to non-pharmaceutically address the trauma of modern life. Help people soar and they'll build their own economic prosperity, thank you. The paternalism of an economic system that first creates economic hardship for millions, then pretends to know how to assuage it, is delusional. Our current economic model is a holdover from an aristocratic perspective that views people as servants to a system; but our economy should be a system that is a servant to the people.

The theory of "trickle-down economics"—the idea that if we give enough of our tax dollars to the already highly paid business sector, then their economic prosperity will trickle down to everyone else—was cast like a modern spell over us during the final two decades of the twentieth century. Given current statistical evidence that most of our propensity for economic success is established in the first eight years of life, if we're really going to subsidize those who "generate prosperity," we should subsidize elementary school teachers!

Businesses that diminish the quality of life and well-being of our citizens do not make us more "prosperous." Are fossil fuel companies and chemical companies engines of prosperity when the damage they cause to our environment increases illness and thus health care costs? Are big agricultural companies engines of prosperity when they wreck our rural economy? Are big pharmaceutical companies engines of prosperity when they knowingly hock unnecessary, addictive medicines for no other reason than to increase their bottom line? Are banks really engines of prosperity when they saddle college students with a lifelong burden of college loans?

All of those industries have the capacity to do good, and in many cases they do. But businesses should have the same ethical obligations to society as any other sector. The idea that a corporation should bear no responsibility to anything other than the financial bottom line of its stockholders destroys the social fabric of our society as well as the natural environment on which all business, and indeed all life, depends.

Those who decry the lack of conscience so rampant in corporate America today are not "antibusiness." Quite the contrary. It is a grand American tradition to resist overreach by the capitalist system when it becomes unmoored from conscience. From the establishment of child labor laws to the rights of workers to unionize to regulations guaranteeing worker safety, corrective measures have been taken to stem capitalism's excesses throughout our history. They are chapters in a grand American narrative. When Franklin Delano Roosevelt pushed for New Deal policies that helped working people and restrained the worst impulses of capitalism, he argued that his policies would save capitalism, not destroy it.

And he was right. The progressive economic conversation is not necessarily about repudiating capitalism, but simply holding it ethically accountable.

The tension between someone's right to make money, on the one hand, and someone else's right to clean air and water, safety, and economic justice, on the other, is built into any free market. What has changed over the last few years, however—primarily because of the undue influence of corporate money on our political system—is how often the government sides with corporate overreach rather than the American people! This change amounts not only to a different economic policy but to a radical realignment of the American government with the interests of its donors as opposed to the interests of its constituency.

In fact, business needs us as much as we need it. Business requires good schools for an educated workforce, just as democracy requires good schools for an educated citizenry. It also requires roads, bridges, and public transit to transport workers and goods. And business needs to have enough people who are doing well to buy its goods and services. Doing things that help people thrive shouldn't be seen as an economic loss but as an economic gain.

We have acquiesced to an aristocratic economic system, lured into doing so not by the tyranny of kings but rather by political propaganda designed to convince the abused that the abuser is their friend. Tax revenue currently given to help the top .01 percent should be used to create the largest matrix of technical colleges and free institutions of higher learning in the world. The fact that our tax revenue is not used this way is a travesty of economic justice and a legacy of ancient serfdom.

The American people have been mentally trained to expect too little from our government. It should not be considered radical that, in the richest nation on earth, our government serves the health and well-being of its citizens before the health and well-being of multibillion-dollar corporations. We need to shift our thinking, and our organizing principles, from an economic to a humanitarian bottom line.

# The Trickle-Down Illusion

America has flourished most when corporations shared the fruits of increased productivity with workers and viewed their ethical obligation as extending beyond mere fiduciary responsibility to stockholders. Between World War II and 1980, we had a vibrant social contract whereby many corporations acted more responsibly toward workers, consumers, and communities. Unions were strong, and workers' wages rose. People earned higher wages and could buy more products, enabling companies to thrive. Prosperity was more broadly shared. From the end of World War II until 1980, corporations in America were expected to consider more than just stockholders to be stakeholders in the company. Employees were considered stakeholders. The community was considered a stakeholder. The environment was considered a stakeholder. Why? Because all of us, not only those who were financially invested, were viewed as having a stake in what happened in corporate America.

After 1980, however, that social contract eroded. Companies shared fewer of the fruits of their labor with workers and pushed to crush unions. Governmentally, the entire decade of the 1980s was a full-scale legitimization of corporate greed. More of a company's wealth went to CEOs and our top 1 percent, weakening our middle class.

The rugged narcissism of Ayn Rand married the greedy free-market-at-the-expense-of-everyone-and-everything-else of Milton Friedman and spawned the financial monster of trickle-down economics. The theory of giving all our money to those who already have enough of it in the hope that through job creation the money will trickle down to everyone else is demonstrably false. Yet that lie has been used in the United States for propaganda purposes for decades, despite all economic evidence to the contrary.

Tax breaks and other financial breaks that favor the wealthiest among us do not create greater prosperity for all; they simply siphon off more and more money to those who already have it and shift more and more money away from those who do not. They do not promote wealth-creation opportunities that benefit all; they simply redistribute wealth from those who do not have much to those who already do. The notion that a $2 trillion tax cut—with 83 cents of every dollar going to the wealthiest among us—is an economic windfall for the people of the United States is nothing short of a cruel hoax perpetrated upon the American people.

If we give a huge amount of money to the rich, we simply don't have enough money left over to help those who are not. This tax bonanza for big business and the very rich drains the public treasury, intensifying pressure to cut vital programs like Social Security, Medicare, and many other social services. An economic model that steals from the American worker on the premise that, once having been stolen, the money will then be returned to them by the thieves who took it in the first place is patently absurd. And one more thing, lest we forget: the workers are supposed to be grateful.

This pattern amounts to more than financial theft; it is an assault on the foundations of our democracy. A government "of the people, by the people, and for the people" is meant to be just that.

A government "of the people, by the people, and for the people" has become a government "of the corporations, by the corporations, and for the corporations." Because huge corporate entities can supply campaign funds way beyond what can be supplied by individual citizens, such industries now exert an influence on government policy that is completely out of proportion to the social—*and* economic—good that they provide. In fact, the 2017 $2 trillion tax cut—which mostly benefited the very wealthy and the largest corporate entities—even removed the tax deduction for public school teachers who use their own money to buy school supplies for their classrooms because school budgets are inadequate!

Corporate interests dominate our politics so much at this point that our government, for all intents and purposes, is merely their handmaiden. Whatever Wall Street wants, Wall Street gets. Corporatism is the new order of the day, and who suffers as a result? *We the people.*

Charles and David Koch, the owners of Koch Industries who pushed most vigorously for the 2017 tax cut, personally received a cut in taxes of $1 billion *a year!* The Koch brothers pledged to spend $400 million in the 2018 election cycle supporting candidates who pushed for the tax bill and promised to continue to extend its economic influence.

In order to pass the bill, the same old trickle-down propaganda was trotted out and sold to ill-informed citizens on the basis that money spent on the tax bill—basically money stolen from the middle class and given to the wealthy—would "trickle down" to the rest of us through job creation, and so forth. But as usual, such propaganda is simply false. In fact, the vast majority of the tax cut money will not go to job creation and wage increases but to extra wealth for the already wealthy. This tax bill is not a reasonable piece of economic legislation; it is a raid on the US Treasury, a massive theft from the American middle and lower classes that will dramatically intensify already extreme income inequality.

According to the Economic Policy Institute, in 1989 the average ratio of CEO to worker compensation was 59 to 1. By 2016, CEO compensation had skyrocketed while typical workers' wages remained fairly stagnant, and the ratio had zoomed to 271 to 1. What this means, then, is that CEOs and stockholders were able to financially benefit from the growth of a company, but its employees could not.

Over the last forty years, CEO compensation has increased 1,070 percent, while the typical worker's compensation has risen only 11 percent; the 2017 tax bill does nothing to assuage that. In fact, it will probably only exacerbate the disparity. Since the bill's passage, big companies, instead of increasing workers' wages, have routinely used the tax cuts for stock buybacks, which simply directs more money to shareholders.

Before the 1980s, CEOs couldn't be paid with stock options; a Reagan-era "reform" changed that, adding an inherent financial conflict to the role of CEO. The CEO of a corporation would thereafter have a financial incentive to increase stock value, often at the expense of larger stakeholder value and the long-term health of the company. Back when our government supported the values of democracy over an obsequious adherence to corporatist demands, corporations had more incentive to do the right thing.

Yet time and time again, Americans are asked to support measures that will aid corporate interests as opposed to their own, the very interests that crucify America's economy and then present themselves as our economic saviors—a brilliant strategy and one that is working. But it will not work forever. In the words of Abraham Lincoln, "You can fool all the people some of the time, some of the people all the time, but you cannot fool all the people all the time." We're in the midst of a new

American awakening, as more and more people realize that a company of thieves is a company of thieves, no matter how mild-mannered, educated, well-spoken, or generous to charity they might be. He who steals billions from the public but then throws a few million to charity is not someone deserving of thanks.

Private giving is important, but so is public fairness. Charity matters, but no amount of private charity can compensate for a basic lack of social justice. Beginning with the Occupy movement, Americans began to see the extraordinary economic disparity between the 1 percent and everyone else. Many now realize that our economy is rigged in favor not only of the 1 percent, but in favor of the 1 percent of the 1 percent. With more and more millennials paying the cost of a rigged system, and simultaneously more and more of them coming of an age to vote, American capitalism will self-correct or it will self-destruct. It is particularly unfair for people who will live the majority of their lives, or even all of their lives, in the twenty-first century to be burdened by the effects of bad economic theories that are outworn leftovers from the late twentieth.

If everyone in America is deemed to have been given by God "the unalienable rights to life, liberty, and the pursuit of happiness," and if, as it says in our Declaration of Independence, "government is instituted among men to secure those rights," then our government should be advocating for *us*, not for corporate conglomerates! It should not be whoring for systems that routinely endanger health, destroy our natural environment, and limit the capacity of those with fewer material resources to thrive.

And we the people have the right to say so.

# History Is on Our Side

Our history is one in which overreach by moneyed forces, more often than not, has ultimately been met by righteous protest. Pushing back against what Thomas Jefferson called "the general tendency of the rich to prey upon the poor" is more in line with the "American way" than our current acquiescence to legalized economic tyranny. America has historically prided itself on expanding economic justice, not weakening it.

The narrative of our past is not one in which Americans consistently folded in the face of economic injustice; it is one in which, more typically, the American people railed against such injustice and ultimately prevailed.

The question of whether capitalism has a moral responsibility to people and the planet is not new. American brilliance applied to business has always been one of our greatest strengths, but we are also a people for whom ethics matters.

Our history has been marked by an ongoing struggle between the engines of economic prosperity, on the one hand, and the ethical considerations that make life meaningful and righteous, on the other. The sacrifice of our moral core to the false god of short-term economic gain is as morally dangerous for our society as it is for an individual. A morality that applies to everything *except* the things that affect real people's daily lives is not morality at all. It is our moral responsibility to insist on just enough regulation of American business and to give enough pushback to an otherwise unfettered, amoral capitalism.

We should neither romanticize the history of capitalism nor fall prey to an intellectually lazy, knee-jerk condemnation of it. We should support it when it supports *us* and push back against its overreach when it becomes untethered from ethical considerations.

That is what Americans have done before, and that is what we should be doing now.

The industrial revolution of the nineteenth and early twentieth centuries brought forth a burst of productivity never before seen, with the industrial prowess of railroads and factories putting America on the path to becoming a major world power. Yet that burst of industrial power induced a financial drunkenness in its main beneficiaries that eventually was met with appropriate, often heroic resistance on the part of both citizens and government. Yes, Henry Ford built the Model T, but he also used a private security force to shoot demonstrators at his factory. Yes, American manufacturing flourished, but it took the passage of child labor laws to make it illegal for six-year-olds to be put to work in factories. Yes, the "robber barons" built great cultural institutions, but they also amassed their enormous wealth by exploiting workers and the environment.

It took the advent of the labor movement, nonprofit organizations, and legislation such as the passage of antitrust legislation and union protections to guarantee a more just economy for all Americans. With the founding of this country, we had already repudiated an economic royalism; we did not, and do not, want to go back to it. Workers should receive fair compensation for the fruits of their labor, and our natural environment should not be desecrated in the name of economic progress. It is those convictions—not the allure of an aristocratic redux—that created the American middle class and made us the wealthiest nation in the world.

After World War II, the GI Bill created by Congress allowed millions of returning soldiers to attend college and enter the workforce at a higher level than they would have otherwise. A nation devastated by World War II then realized that our biggest opportunity for an economic re-greening lay in educating the American population and rebuilding our infrastructure. This civic wisdom led to an explosion of economic prosperity among us and the creation of America's great middle class.

An extreme corporatist agenda—increasingly hostile to democracy itself—has worked hard over the last few years to interrupt that pattern and change America's course. It has worked hard to diminish the power of unions, reduce the progressive nature of the tax system, undermine the effectiveness of regulatory agencies, and slash spending on programs like public housing and other aid to the poor. All of these actions have contributed mightily to increased wealth inequality and other economic and social injustices experienced by the working poor as well as those without work. Most recently, corporatist forces represented on the Supreme Court have even chipped away at the Voting Rights Act, diminishing the power of the people most affected by those injustices to fight back against them.

The new corporatist extremism has come at us with such shock and awe over the last few decades that our resistance to it has sometimes been fragmented and unfocused. Like a boxer hit right in the eyes, we've been knocked back so hard that, seeing stars, we've been unable at first to adequately respond. And at other times, after being hit again and again, we have simply grown too weak to hit back. But knowing our history can create the emotional support we need to get back into the game. It's almost as though we can hear our ancestors exhorting us, "Get up! Don't let this happen! Fix it!"

A fundamental shift in the functioning of our government—from primarily serving the financial interests of a small group of corporate entities to once again making the interests of the people of the United States its highest priority—is the course-correction now needed.

The average American isn't asking for gifts from Santa Claus; he or she is asking for simple fairness and decency and respect. The values of brotherhood and justice that form the framework of any right relationship form the framework of a healthy society. And that applies to the economy too.

Millions in America today—hardworking people who should have every right to feel securely ensconced in the middle class—are only one unfortunate step away from the ranks of the poor. They know that a health crisis, a car accident, or a layoff could ruin them financially. Their anger and despair are valid.

An unfettered global capitalism, untethered to any ethical considerations beyond its fiduciary responsibility to stockholders, is both a political and spiritual abomination. Any system that lacks compassion, love, and conscience is out of alignment with the moral laws of the universe and in time will produce chaos.

It is spiritual voices that should decry such injustice—and often do. In his 2013 exhortation on global capitalism, Pope Francis said:

> *While the earnings of the minority are growing exponentially, so, too, is the gap separating the majority from the prosperity enjoyed by those happy few. The imbalance is the result of ideologies which defend the absolute autonomy of the marketplace and financial speculation. . . . A new tyranny is thus born, invisible and often virtual, which relentlessly*

*imposes its own laws and rules. . . . The thirst for power and possessions knows no limits. In this system, which tends to devour everything that stands in the way of increased profits, whatever is fragile, like the environment, is defenseless before the interests of a deified market, which become the only rule.* *

A new economic ethos, one aligned with a consciousness not only of prosperity but also of justice, not only of wealth-creation but also of deep democracy, is rising up among the people of the United States and the people of the world. This represents an unstoppable force that the American capitalist enterprise would do best to work with, and not against. Otherwise it will create its own repudiation. Someone once said that if we want things to stay the same, then some things are going to have to change.

---

* Pope Francis, *The Joy of the Gospel: Evangelii Gaudium* (Vatican City: Libreria Editrice Vaticana, 2013).

# Money in Service to Love

And now for the good news!

Fortunately, many corporate leaders in America today are enlightened thinkers. Some are working daily to transform the capitalist ethos, putting it back on track with the angels of our better nature. In a 2018 interview with the *New York Times*, for instance, the fashion mogul Eileen Fisher said that she believed stock sharing with employees should be mandatory. "I think corporations should have to share a minimum 10 percent of their profits with the people working. It's not socialism; it's good for business."*

Fisher is not alone among successful American business leaders who are turning the tide toward corporate responsibility. Whole Foods CEO John Mackey has founded a movement called "conscious capitalism," calling upon corporate leaders to reintroduce ethics and values into corporate governance. In the summer of 2018, the Danone Corporation, a multibillion-dollar global company that acquired American Whitewave Food, converted its entire corporate structure to a B-Corporation (or B-Corp.). A B-Corp. bases its success on

---

* David Gelles, "Eileen Fisher: 'When Was Fashion Week?'" *New York Times*, October 5, 2018.

social and environmental performance, going beyond profit maximization. It holds itself both publicly and privately accountable to a higher ethical standard. Danone is joining a group of conscious capitalist firms that have outperformed their public counterparts by a factor of ten to one as measured by stock valuation.

An argument for a loving economy isn't an argument against the free market; if anything, it's an argument for letting more people into its ranks. This argument recognizes that what is free to many of us is not free at all to millions of people who are locked out of the "free market" entirely.

How many young Americans whose lives are stymied by the burden of thousands of dollars in college loans would love nothing more than to have the cash on hand to start their own small businesses? How many hardworking Americans, trapped in one or even more low-paying jobs, have the talent and ability, as well as the desire, to be creating, producing, and contributing to America's consumer base—if only they had a chance?

All of us know, deep in our hearts, that a good life for everyone is a better life for everyone. Not every rich person is greedy any more than every poor person is noble and pure. A politics of love in America doesn't speak to the part of us that is rich or poor, but to the part of us that is American.

We don't just need small, random acts of love today. We need huge, strategized acts of doing the right thing. I don't believe that God simply wants us to be good people; I believe God wants us to be a good nation. Not just personally but also politically, we should care. And I believe that deep in our hearts, most of us do.

In truth, a moral argument is not incompatible with an economic argument, because aligning with a higher natural order is never to humanity's detriment. The universe of love is a universe of plenty. After World War II, millions of veterans were able to go to college because of the GI Bill, which also made low-interest mortgages available to expand home-ownership, and President Eisenhower's administration built the interstate highway system. These government actions, by making deep investments in the bottom line of bettering the lives of human beings, helped create the healthiest economy America has ever had.

## Love and Wealth Inequality

There is no real mystery as to what created the wealth inequality that's now higher in this country than at any time since 1929. The systematic removal of American wealth from the middle and lower classes to the very richest among us has been happening for decades.

At this point, the wealthiest 1 percent of American households own 40 percent of the country's wealth. The three richest people in the United States have as much money as the bottom half of all Americans.

The problem, of course, is not that some people are rich. As Americans, we celebrate the opportunity for wealth-creation among hardworking people. The problem is not with individuals, but with an unfair system. The problem is that our laws are skewed in such a way as to make it easier for the rich to stay rich and get richer, and harder for those who are not rich to rise above their circumstances. The system now makes it unnecessarily harder for average Americans to break the material chains that bind them.

Currently, the driving impulse behind policies emanating from three political power centers—the White House, the Senate, and the Supreme Court—is to favor the financial viability of large corporations at the expense of their workers. The current argument over net neutrality is just such an issue, with our newest Supreme Court justice, Brett Kavanaugh, having argued that net neutrality laws—which ensure that everyone has the same access to the internet—would be a violation of *corporations'* First Amendment rights!

That's the face of a government that puts corporations before people. The elite use government statistics to brag about how many jobs they've created, but more and more of those jobs are low-paying rather than middle-class jobs. And the low-paying job sector in America does not routinely pave the way for growth opportunity, but rather is increasingly an economic trap in which millions of people are forced to rely on public assistance while their corporate overlords earn obscene amounts of wealth.

More than 50 percent of employees in the fast-food industry rely on some kind of public assistance. The co-owner of Burger King has a net worth of $25 billion, while his workers receive an estimated $356 million in public subsidies every year. And once again, those subsidies are paid for by you and me. McDonald's, with a net worth of more than $104 billion, actually encourages its workers to sign up for public assistance. It's *our* money that pays for food stamps, Medicaid, and public housing, so that some McDonald's workers can put food on their tables.

According to one report, in 2014, Walmart employees received billions in public aid. How does that jibe with the fact that the Walton family, which owns Walmart, is the wealthiest family in the country, with an estimated net worth reported at somewhere around $130 billion?

Jeff Bezos, worth an estimated $158 billion, bowed to public pressure and increased the wages of all US workers at Amazon to $15 an hour after Senator Bernie Sanders introduced a bill that would have taxed Amazon for the amount that we, the US taxpayers, were billed in public assistance to his underpaid workers. Bezos's move is not without controversy, however, since some Amazon workers will lose benefits, including stock options.

Ideally, when it comes to increasing the minimum wage, more corporations will follow suit and raise wages as Bezos did. Until then, the rest of us will continue to foot the bill for the failure of some billionaires to pay their workers fair wages. The cost to taxpayers of increased public assistance to these workers is so high, in fact, that the very purveyors of the unjust system are champing at the bit to start cutting the government entitlement programs that make it possible for many people to simply live.

There are a few American politicians struggling to right the ship of American capitalism by using the powers of government to advocate for the right of every American to simple economic justice. In addition to a bill sponsored by Senator Bernie Sanders to charge huge corporations the amount of money we're having to pay in federal assistance to the employees they routinely underpay, Senator Elizabeth Warren has also introduced legislation to encourage greater corporate responsibility. Called the Accountable Capitalism Act, this bill aims to restore some of the social responsibility that many companies showed for several decades following World War II.

The idea that the role of our government is to advocate for the economic aristocrat rather than the right of the average American to pursue his or her happiness is contrary to everything this country is supposed to stand for. It is bad economics, and it is bad for democracy. The God-given "unalienable rights to life, liberty, and the pursuit of happiness" should include economic fairness.

There are good politicians who see what has happened and are trying to change it. There are good corporate leaders who see what has happened and are trying to change it. There are good social and political activists who see what has happened and are trying to change it.

It's time for the rest of us to weigh in.

# 5

# AMERICAN YOUTH
## EQUAL RIGHTS FOR ANGELS

Often when I look at a small child, I feel like I'm looking at an angel.

Yet if children are angels, as a country we're sure not treating them that way. Unseen by most of us, America has a terrible underbelly of millions of suffering children. Health crisis. Hunger crisis. Addiction crisis. Safety crisis. Education crisis. Traumatic stress crisis. So many of America's children are endangered either physically or emotionally, it should be seen as a humanitarian emergency.

Obviously, the problem isn't that we don't love our children. But the love that will save the world is not just love for our own children. It is also love for children on the other side of town and the other side of the world. For every problem, whether personal or societal, the solution lies in the realization of our oneness and the expansion of our love.

The economic system of the United States was invented at a time when women did not yet have a public voice. The care of children was considered "women's work." But today we do have a voice, and it should be raised loudly on behalf of every woman's child. Women have a unique role to play in addressing what is in essence systemic child neglect.

It took more than a hundred years of feminism to root out of Western consciousness the idea that women are the property of men. But in the arduous struggle for women's equality over the years, perhaps we did not attend enough to the concomitant needs of children to be freed from the yoke of ancient injustices. While we have evolved as a society beyond the idea that women are the property of men, we have not fully evolved beyond the notion that children are the property of adults.

Children are not our property. They have their own rights of citizenship. If a child is a born or naturalized citizen of the United States, then he or she is legally accorded all the rights thereof.

If every citizen is given by God unalienable rights to "life, liberty, and the pursuit of happiness," then government theoretically owes children more, not less, than adults because adults can more fully provide for themselves. A small child cannot feed, clothe, or educate himself or herself. Children cannot vote against special interests that profit financially off activities that harm their health, or that deny them education through the leeching of financial resources, or that profit off their problems through unjust punishment.

Few people want to actively harm a child, and there is certainly a universal consensus among us that such behavior should not be tolerated. We are certainly willing to hold an individual accountable for hurting one child. But as a society, we are neglecting millions of them. Most Americans probably don't appreciate the level of chronic trauma now suffered by children in our midst.

Due mainly to economically disadvantaged parents, millions of American children live in food-insecure households, lacking consistent access to sufficient and nutritious food. Millions of our children go to school each day in schools that do not meet safety standards. Almost four million children lack health care coverage. Millions go to schools where there are not the required school supplies to reasonably expect a child to learn to read. And when children can't learn to read by eight years old, the chances of them graduating from high school are greatly reduced and the chances of incarceration are increased.

And what are they to do? They are not old enough to vote; therefore they have no voter influence. They're not old enough to work; therefore they have no financial leverage. They can't afford highly paid lobbyists to stroll the halls of Congress to advocate on their behalf. Who is to speak for them, if not us?

And that is why politics matters. It's not something "over there" to people whose lives must bear the impact of policies that work against their interests every day. An issue shouldn't spark us only if it happens to impact us personally. Politics shouldn't be just about you and yours, or me and mine. It's about we and ours. Politics is the purview of our collective sensibilities and our collective decision-making. It should be a place where we address more than just what we want for ourselves; it should be a place where we come together to consider what is right for America. There's a bigger question in life than "How am I doing?" And that's "How are *we* doing?"

Millions of children living in chronic distress in the richest country in the world is a form of collective child neglect. And that should matter to all of us.

# The Cost of Chronic Trauma

The crisis of American children is multidimensional, with manifestations in our economic system, health system, educational system, justice system, and mental health care system.

Seventy-eight percent of incarcerated inmates in America came out of the child welfare system. Sex trafficking of American girls is a $91 billion business, making us number one among sex-trafficking countries around the world. Some 120,000 girls were shipped into Minneapolis for last year's Super Bowl, making it arguably the largest sex-trafficking event in the world.

Obviously, the primary problem here cannot be reduced to any one issue. Poverty is a problem. Opioids are a problem. The breakdown of the family is a problem. The ease with which fathers can avoid making child care payments is a problem. Lack of education, particularly among low-income populations, is a problem. An increase in the number of children sent to foster care is a problem. The fact that the sex-trafficking industry has infiltrated the network of foster-care parents and even hovers over schools is a problem. But perhaps the worst problem of all is how desensitized we are to the urgency of the problem.

More children have been killed by gunfire in the United States since the 2012 mass shooting at Sandy Hook Elementary School in Newtown, Connecticut, than American soldiers have been killed in overseas combat since 9/11. From sex trafficking to a chronic pattern of school shootings to children torn from their parents' arms as an act of immigration policy to millions of children living in chronic trauma, something has gone horribly wrong. And what child can stand up for himself or herself and say, "Enough is enough"?

Our system does not actively transgress against children. For the most part, the American legal system does its best to protect children from active measures that harm their well-being, though far too few resources are devoted to that purpose, to be sure. In a country whose government has increasingly aligned itself with the interests of corporate power before the needs of its people, it should surprise no one that the interests of children fall to the lowest spot on our political priority list. Teachers' unions, youth advocacy groups, and nonprofit educational organizations such as the Children's Defense Fund do important work, but they're no match for the economic clout accorded to corporate interests.

The vital interests of children should be seen as our most important, not our least important, political concern—and then treated that way. We should massively realign the material resources of our country in the direction of children eight years old and younger. If we were thinking about genuine long-range economic planning—not to mention securing the rights of life, liberty, and the pursuit of happiness to every citizen—then there would be not one American in early childhood with anything less than the best-quality health care, the best-quality education, the best-quality access to the arts, and the best-quality food.

Why should a child's basic rights as an American be tended to less just because the circumstances of his or her birth were less fortunate? Where in our Constitution does it say that rich children should have greater access to the fruits of liberty? If we're going to take the "God gave all men inalienable rights to life, liberty, and the pursuit of happiness" part of the Declaration of Independence and declare it no longer operative, if we're going to take the "governments are instituted among men to secure those rights" phrase and simply declare it null and void, then shouldn't we at least have a conversation about it first?

We're the only country in the world that funds our educational system through property taxes, guaranteeing that children of well-to-do parents have a good chance of a quality education while children of less-well-to-do parents do not. It is astonishing to look online and see all the ways in which teachers ask for help getting their students basic school supplies, just so that they can learn. This points out a basic flaw in our political perspective: care for our children should not be a *charity* issue, but a *justice* issue. And at the deepest level, a human issue.

It's grossly cynical to tell people to climb the ladder of success when, as children, they weren't put onto the first rung by those who are older. As Martin Luther King Jr. would say, you can't tell someone to pull themselves up by their bootstraps when they don't even have any boots. Often we read of people who "escaped" a childhood of poverty in America, but all of us should ask ourselves: in the richest nation in the world, why should so many children be in need of "escape"?

The health and well-being of American children should be top on our list of national priorities. The means of self-actualization through education and culture should be available to every child, regardless of what neighborhood they live in. Their libraries should be fully funded temples of arts and literacy. Their schools should be palaces of learning and joy. Their neighborhoods should all have safe and beautiful parks for them to play in.

To ask for those things doesn't mean we're asking for too much. Not asking for them means we are asking for too little. There is no lack of money to do this. This is simply too much money going elsewhere.

Americans have become so habituated to skewed natural priorities that we're almost programmed to ask, "But where would the money come from?"

"How would we pay for all that education and culture, health and safety?" ask those who have no problem whatsoever paying for ill-begotten wars and tax cuts for the extremely wealthy. Such a question should be met by laughter from those who were never consulted as to how we would pay for a $2 trillion war in Iraq (which, among other things, created ISIS) or a $2 trillion tax cut for the wealthiest among us (which, among other things, is already adding to our wealth inequality).

Let's ask instead what price we're paying by not doing more to help our children. Or to be more exact, the price that our children are paying and will continue to pay. When it comes to our children, we should protect them from the ravages of poverty no differently than we would protect them from the ravages of a natural disaster.

According to the most recent poverty data from the US Census Bureau, almost 13 million children in the United States lived in poverty in 2017. Most of those children went to school hungry each day. Hunger diminished both their capacity to learn and the statistical probability of their future success, both educationally and professionally.

If everyone who reads this will simply put down your book for a moment, close your eyes, and try to imagine what it means that 13 million children in this country go to school hungry each day, then we will be a better nation for it.

In her book *On Becoming*, Michelle Obama describes in some detail the admirable efforts she made while living in the East Wing on behalf of America's disadvantaged children. I couldn't help wondering while reading it, however, why the plight of those children didn't get more attention in the West Wing.

In the words of Nelson Mandela, "There can be no keener revelation of a society's soul than the way in which it treats its children." Yet the United States ranks at the bottom, or near the bottom, on almost every indicator when it comes to governmental policies toward children. In the United States, youth homicide rates are more than ten times the rates of other leading industrialized nations. Social scientists and psychologists describe our own "war zones"—areas in some of our more violently charged homes, communities, and inner cities—where levels of trauma and post-traumatic stress among children are similar to those experienced by returning vets. But there is nothing "post" about their traumatic stress, because it is triggered and retriggered every day. We have simply normalized their despair.

Americans have become enamored of the idea that our government should be run like a business, but that idea is flawed. In fact, our problem is that too often our government *is* run like a business—the wrong kind of business. It gives precedence to the gains of corporate shareholders while often ignoring the needs of the average stakeholder, which in this case is every citizen. And what business can long endure that pays out dividends to its shareholders but ignores the development of new products?

The US government should not be run like a business; it should be run like a family. Millions of years of evolution prove that no natural system can survive and thrive that does not first take care of its young. New Zealand's prime minister, Jacinda Ahern, in a speech to the United Nations in 2018, said that her goal is to make her country the best place in the world to be a child. Americans should ask for no less.

Over 74 million people in the United States are under the age of eighteen.* And every one of them could have a world-class education, starting in preschool and going through college or technical school. Every dollar spent on the health, education, and general welfare of our young will multiply mightily in the form of the creativity, health, and economic vitality of the adults they will become. And every dollar we withhold from them is stolen many times over from our economy and social vitality in the future.

The relative neglect of the needs of this segment of our population is a threat to the security of our country, because

---

* Lindsay M. Howden and Julie A. Meyer, "Age and Sex Composition: 2010," *2010 Census Briefs,* US Census Bureau C2010BR-03 (May 2011), https://www.census.gov/prod/cen2010/briefs/c2010br-03.pdf.

it is a threat to our future. How dare those of us who do not statistically stand to be around in fifty years live our lives in such a way as to make the lives of those who will still be here more difficult? Such thinking derives from an economic system that views children as dispensable because they add no immediate economic value to that system. It is true that they add no short-term value to our economy, but they are critical to the long-term possibility of survival—the survival not only of our democracy, but possibly of life on earth.

# Investing in New Beginnings

I n Proverbs 22:6, it is written, "Start children off in the way they should go, and even when they are old they will not turn from it." This is not just a religious scripture; it is a scientific fact. There is no greater human potential than that provided by the brain capacity and neuroplasticity of children under the age of eight. We now know in ways that were not scientifically established a century ago that a child's brain is infinitely more flexible, more emotionally intelligent, and more capable of learning and retaining information than an adult's.

As the iconic filmmaker Billy Wilder once said, "If you have a problem with the third act, the real problem is in the first act." The most sophisticated kind of long-term planning focuses on getting things right at the beginning.

This country is standing on top of millions of tiny gold mines. Enter any kindergarten and you'll see an unlimited amount of unmined energy, creativity, and genius. Every American elementary school student has potential talent and intelligence unmatched by any technological, financial, or institutional power. Nothing humanity has created can begin to rival the potential of the human brain, and no human brain carries more potential than the brain of the child. The greatest fuel for twenty-first-century abundance comes not from the oil or gas in our ground, but from the genius in our elementary schools.

Our political system is the product of a time when children were basically thought of as little adults-in-waiting. The fields of psychology, neurology, and sociology are relatively new compared to the economic and social theorizing from which our modern society emerged. Stuck in twentieth-century and even nineteenth-century models of social theorizing, we've viewed children as charges to be taken care of, yet never factoring their intellectual, emotional, cultural, and physical development into our long-term view of progress. The beginning of any system is all-important, and that is what childhood *is*—not only for an individual but for a society. Once a beginning is set, things are far more difficult to change afterwards. In its low rankings on prenatal care, maternal health, and the psychological and emotional care of new parents, the US government fails not only mothers and children but also the country at large.

We're one of very few advanced democracies, for instance, that don't provide federally funded parental leave. It's ironic that this failure stems from sectors of the business community insisting that they can't afford it; in fact, the time spent by a newborn child in the arms of a parent statistically increases the child's productivity in later years, as well as the parent's productivity when they return to work unencumbered by the sadness of going back to work too soon. The idea of helping people has been propagandistically turned into some twisted vision of a nanny state—like it's some enabling, codependent, fuzzy-minded thinking as opposed to what it really is: action that aligns us with our spiritual nature, the laws of the universe, and the ultimate well-being of all.

As long as there was a dearth of women in positions of political, social, and economic power, this chronic skewing of American priorities in the direction of short-term economic interests as opposed to humanitarian values was understandable. As long as women were basically invisible, children were invisible as well. But women are invisible no longer, and neither should our children be.

Of course, we should teach our children reading, writing, and arithmetic. But our educational system should expand to include a more whole-person vision of what it takes to prepare a child for self-actualized life in the twenty-first century. We should help our children develop the emotional and psychological skills to navigate life in what has become an extremely complex world. Until we do that, our educational system will remain inadequate despite whatever funding we put into it.

Are we preparing American children to grow up to be cogs in the wheel of a vast economic machine—designed to protect the advantaged ones, picking out the most talented ones to fill the ranks of the elite—or are we committed to the development of the full potential of every child to be their most creative, empowered best? The former—basically the educational model we follow now—is the legacy of an aristocratic worldview, while the latter is the actualization of democracy.

We should do more than educate children so they're prepared to get a job. We should educate children so they're prepared for greatness. We should educate them to realize that each of them has the potential to be anyone and anything they want, and that their opportunities are limitless. *That* is the American Dream.

Every child in America could have a world-class education, starting in preschool and going through college or technical school. No American child should go to a school in which class size makes teaching more a matter of crowd control than the cultivation of young minds. Every American child should learn civics and history, for only then are they adequately prepared for the responsibility of citizen leadership in a democracy.

Children should be taught not only what to think—as in science and math—but also *how* to think, as in honing their critical thought processes so they know how to think for themselves. America's educational system should be the crown jewel of America's investment portfolio, our greatest asset in producing creativity and progress. In the words of the poet William Butler Yeats, "Education is not the filling of a pail, but the lighting of a fire."

# Demanding Change

A kindergartener in a disadvantaged neighborhood has the same inner fire as a kindergartener in an advantaged neighborhood. No child in America should be denied a world-class education because his or her parents are poor. Such disparity perpetuates our slide toward a veiled aristocratic system. Access to the finest education remaining in the hands of a few is the way an unjust system ensures that *power* remains in the hands of a few. That's why the failure to provide the highest-quality education to *every* American child is a passive attack on our democracy.

Millions of American children, born as innocent children of God with unlimited human potential, fall through the cracks in our society ever year. They do so without the level of support they need to function as healthy, productive members of society, neglected not just by their families but by our society. Failure to provide this support drives up the incidence of violence, drug addiction, and other dysfunctions among our young people, only adding to the size and entrenchment of America's permanent underclass. And how do we pay for that? With our blood and treasure.

Children growing up in homes riddled by trauma—much of it the result of the scourge of poverty and racism—are likely to be clinically diagnosable with mental health disorders. The high statistical probability of their taking a path along what the author Marion Wright Edelman, founder of the Children's Defense Fund, has termed the "cradle to prison" pipeline is a moral scourge upon our country. When the richest nation in the world fails to address the hunger in the stomachs of its children and the hunger for learning in their minds, we as a nation are in danger of reaping desperate consequences.

Are we not already? Of the incarcerated 2.3 million Americans—more per capita than any other nation in the world—does any serious person think this represents only personal failure on the part of those imprisoned? Is there nothing there for us to look at as a society, not only in terms of our criminal justice system but also in terms of our failure to prepare more of our children for a productive, successful life?

We the people can rise up and stand for a massive change. Trauma-informed education and community wraparound services are needed and should be adequately funded. From playgrounds to parks to libraries, from better-paid teachers to upgraded schools, from music to dance to art, from social and emotional learning schools to nonviolent communication skills, from health care and mindfulness techniques to whole-family support services, we should upgrade our commitment to children not just a little, not just incrementally, but fundamentally. Most important, we should connect the dots between economic disadvantage as it affects a parent and the almost inevitable trauma it imposes on a child. With nearly a third of all Americans living in near-poverty conditions, you don't have to be an economist to know that something is wrong with this picture.

The economic formulas of a bygone era are morally neutral and essentially heartless. They leave out women, they leave out mothering, they leave out children, and they leave out love.

No wonder we're so fractured as a society, given that we're so fractured from our own essential nature. No system thrives that doesn't prepare its continuation. We're a generation more aware of our own childhood wounds than any generation before, yet neglectful of the multiple wounds to the hearts and minds and bodies of America's children today. Only when we awaken spiritually to our responsibility to our young will we be creating a more sustainable future. By allowing so many desperate children to wallow in despair, we're creating a future in which we will inevitably be wallowing in our own.

What's impressive about American young people is that despite the odds that are pitted against so many of them, they continue to strive for the American Dream. What all of us should ask ourselves is why our society is invested in making it so hard. Governmental action should help people thrive, not make it more difficult for them to do so.

About 40 million Americans hold student loans, and about 70 percent of bachelor's degree recipients graduate with debt.* The size of student debt is staggering, with 44 million people owing $1.5 trillion in student loans. Most of those loans are held by the federal government, which could ameliorate those debts if it chose. Instead, it has essentially created among America's youth a new form of bondage that exists only because our young are trying to better themselves. The average student in the class of 2016 graduated with a student loan debt of between $28,000 and $37,000. Millions of young Americans would love nothing more than to participate in a free-market economy by having enough discretionary spending money to build a website and start their own company. How ironic that our capitalist system now works so hard to keep them out, when all they want is just a chance to be let in!

Nothing holds more promise for the twenty-first century than a radical rethinking of our responsibility to children and young adults. This country should undertake a massive realignment of our resources in the direction of the young. We should make college or technical school available to everyone. We should cancel most college debts. And why should we do all these things? To unshackle the American spirit, to release

---

* Kaitlin Mulhere, "A Shocking Number of Americans Now Owe at Least $50,000 in Student Debt—and Many Aren't Paying It Down," *Money,* February 22, 2018, http://time.com/money/5169145/50000-dollars-student-debt-default/.

the chains that bind our circumstances, to liberate the potential in every citizen . . . and then to watch this country soar! America's problem is the problem of a constricted heart. As individuals we are a good and decent people, but as a society we have become rather mean. It is time to reconsider. It is time to self-correct.

# 6

# RACE AND REPENTANCE

## OUT OF MANY, ONE

From a spiritual perspective, if our life is in crisis, we can repair it only by getting straight with God. And we cannot get straight with God without getting straight with each other. It is our God-given purpose on earth to love one another, and no serious spiritual path gives any of us a pass on making the effort.

No one always gets everything right, and neither does any country. Sometimes people and countries can do bad things. But the atonement principle, universal to all serious spiritual systems, posits the power of repentance. We can atone for our mistakes, make meaningful amends, and behave differently going forward. No life, and no country, can redeem itself otherwise.

The law of cause and effect, or what in the East is called *karma*, is the spiritual principle that organizes the universe. It is an unalterable law that every cause will create an effect; love calls forth love, and lovelessness calls forth lovelessness. Only through atonement and amends can this law be overridden. We can change things on the level of effect over and over, but only when we change things on the level of cause are they fundamentally altered. We must change our thinking as well as our behavior in order to change our lives.

A politics of love recognizes that the same spiritual, emotional, and psychological principles that prevail in an individual's life also prevail in a nation's. There is no opening our hearts to God without opening our hearts to each other, for our God-given purpose on the earth is to love one another. We feel blessed when we choose to bless others, and we cannot feel blessed when we withhold our blessing from others. We cannot find God outside our relationship to each other. It's our sacred task as citizens to take a deeper look at America's "relationship issues." That means not only our relationships with other nations but also our relationships with each other.

The United States, like many other countries, has relationship conflicts that literally go back hundreds of years. In addition to the relationship between white Americans of European ancestry and Native Americans, whose ancestors inhabited this land for thousands of years before white settlers got here, our primary domestic relationship is the relationship between white Americans and black descendants of slaves who were brought to this continent from Africa.

I do not believe the average American is racist, but I do believe the average American is woefully undereducated about our racial history, particularly since the Civil War. Have we taken strides forward since the days of slavery? Yes. But have we completed the task of reconciliation between the races? Not anywhere near. In fact, in some ways over the last fifty years we have been sliding backwards. Our generation needs to educate ourselves more deeply, and act more nobly, in order to realize not only where we've been but also where we should be going.

A politics of love is a whole-person pursuit that traces the psychological as well as political history of a relationship between peoples. Only when we know that history can we understand an issue deeply enough to adequately address it.

Slavery existed in slave-owning states in America beginning in the 1600s, and it increased significantly with the expansion of the cotton industry in the early 1800s. It did not end until the passage of the Thirteenth Amendment in 1865. When finally freed, the slave population in America was somewhere around four million.

On April 9, 1865, Confederate general Robert E. Lee surrendered to Union general Ulysses S. Grant at the courthouse in Appomattox, Virginia. Thus, the Civil War ended.

The stroke of a presidential signature on the Emancipation Proclamation, even an amendment to the Constitution, could abolish an institution but not the pathology that produced it. For external remedies do not of themselves eradicate internal causes. Racist thought burrowed even more deeply into the fabric of Southern society after the Civil War. For most Americans today, it is our racial history *since* the Civil War that remains misunderstood.

During the Reconstruction Era from 1865 to 1877, with federal troops stationed throughout the region, a vanquished South was forced to come to terms with having lost the war. Lincoln's voice proclaiming "malice towards none, and charity for all" had been silenced forever, and Northern attitudes were far from compassionate toward the defeated South. Bitterness over having had to fight the war was the main emotional tone of the North, and humiliation over having lost it was the main emotional tone of the South.

Upon the removal of federal troops at the end of the Reconstruction Era, many Southerners created forms of institutionalized oppression to express their hatred toward former slaves. The postwar period saw the rise of an era of white supremacy in the American South that was almost as ugly as slavery itself. Violence against blacks did not end so much as morph into other forms, both personal and institutional. Many former slave owners had simply held their breath during the period of Reconstruction, waiting until federal troops were gone before seeking their revenge. They had not awakened to the deep humanity of African Americans; they simply could no longer own them.

Although the field of psychology did not exist in the nineteenth century, we can now look back at this time with a much deeper understanding of the emotional as well as political forces that were at work at the time. That former slaves were now fellow citizens represented not only a change in circumstances but a fundamental change in social relationships. *We used to be rich and you were slaves on our plantations; now we are poor, we have nothing, and you are free living here among us.* History doesn't unfold only according to what happens on the outside, but every bit as much according to what happens on the inside.

The South hadn't given up slavery voluntarily; it gave it up for one reason only—that it lost the war. They thus surrendered their slaves but not their anger. The last thing the former slave-owner class of Southerners was ready to do for a population they had kicked to the ground for hundreds of years was to say, "Great, now let's be friends." A cold and cruel dehumanization of black people before the war was replaced with hot and violent rage after it ended.

Had Lincoln lived, things might have unfolded very differently. But in the absence of enlightened leadership, the ugliest faces of both the North and the South prevailed after the Civil War. Groups such as the Ku Klux Klan, founded in the 1860s, began a wave of terror in which lynchings— hangings of black Americans as well as of whites seeking to help them, carried out by angry mobs of white Americans— became common. Once federal troops were withdrawn from the Southern states in 1877 and white supremacists regained control of Southern state legislatures, blacks were routinely intimidated and attacked to prevent their voting in state and federal elections.

Even as early as 1865 and 1866, laws called the Black Codes were passed in Southern states to restrict the freedom of African Americans and keep them tied to a subpar labor economy. During the period between 1890 and 1908, Southern legislatures also passed constitutions and electoral rules guaranteed to disenfranchise most blacks and many poor whites. Racist legislatures enacted a series of segregation and Jim Crow laws to enforce the second-class citizenship status of black Americans. Lynching and election violence became normal, reaching a peak in the late nineteenth and early twentieth centuries.

While most people realize the evils of slavery, many may not realize the extent to which social, economic, and political barriers prevented the integration into free society of the formerly enslaved population *after* the Civil War.

If you've kicked someone to the ground, you need to do more than just stop kicking; you have a moral responsibility to help them get back up. You can't just say to four million people who have had no experience other than that of forced labor, "Glad you're free! Now good luck to ya! Hope you find a good job!" What they were freed *to* was a violent prejudice, white supremacy, and segregation that would go unchallenged in any fundamental way for another hundred years. Thousands of black Americans fled to Northern cities in search of jobs and freedom denied them where they came from, yet racial prejudice routinely met them even there.

It was not until the mid-1950s and the 1960s that the horrors of segregation were met, challenged, and resisted by the Reverend Dr. Martin Luther King Jr. and the civil rights movement. The struggle of the civil rights movement was a heroic repudiation of racist oppression, and Dr. King became the target, both professionally and personally, of the full force of supremacist rage. From the lynching of integration rights workers to police brutality to church bombings and ultimately the murder of Dr. King, the white supremacist movement did not go down quietly.

Yet the movement prevailed. Dr. King was a Baptist preacher whose moral authority matched his towering intellect and political acumen. He realized that the movement's political strategy had to be matched by its spiritual authority in order to awaken the conscience of a nation. Having gone to India and studied the nonviolent philosophy of Mahatma Gandhi, King applied the principles of nonviolence to the struggle for civil rights back in the United States. As a minister and then as a movement leader, King had the Gandhian "soul force" necessary to lead his people to the promised land of racial justice. It was not only the things he said but the things he did that parted the waters of racial hatred. Not only did he *believe* that love is the only force powerful enough to overcome hate; Dr. King displayed that love with the full force of his being. His combination of nonviolence and political courage stirred a nation that had long acquiesced to the ugliness of white supremacy, and under his leadership the civil rights movement created the political will to pass federal civil rights legislation.

After so much horror and bloodshed, Dr. King and others who struggled so valiantly beside him achieved a historic political victory. The Civil Rights Act of 1964 ended segregation in public places and banned employment discrimination on the basis of race, color, religion, sex, or national origin; the Voting Rights Act of 1965 prohibited racial discrimination in voting.

As someone who grew up in Texas, I can remember many of the outward signs of segregation in America. I'm aware of the vast strides that have been taken toward the creation of racial justice. But as a student of history, I also know how much remains to be done and how in some ways we're even sliding backwards. Mass incarceration means we're sliding backwards. Racial disparity in criminal sentencing means we're sliding backwards. Voter suppression efforts aimed primarily at disenfranchised populations means we're sliding backwards. While we shouldn't minimize the struggle, sacrifices, and victories of our ancestors, neither should we pretend that we've come further than we have. For reasons external as well as internal, the establishment of full justice for African Americans remains a task not yet completed.

# An Unfinished Task

The hot violence of slavery was replaced by the burrowing violence of white supremacy, which was finally vanquished by the victories of the civil rights movement. The mistake many white Americans make is to think the story ended there. Indeed, after the civil rights movement America's complicated racial history continued. And for all the talk about trauma these days, we would do well to consider the psychological trauma of hundreds of years of oppression.

What came next—after a nation exhausted by the social and political tumult of the 1960s elected Richard Nixon president in 1968—was a cold but insidious violence called "benign neglect." Benign neglect is a phrase first articulated by Daniel Patrick Moynihan, then Nixon's urban affairs adviser. Moynihan argued that the drama of the civil rights movement should be followed by a period of social quiet in the relationship between blacks and whites. It was not necessarily a proactively racist sentiment on Moynihan's part, or even on Nixon's. But it legitimized an abandonment of any effort to continue the pursuit of racial justice, and in that sense at least it was a passive betrayal of the relationship on the part of white America. Benign neglect sent the message that the government wasn't going to intentionally hurt you, but that if you were being hurt by someone else, it was not going to proactively help you either. And in too many ways, that is where we remain.

While it was one generation's job to end slavery, and another generation's job to pass civil rights legislation, it is our generation's job to address the fact that today, over 150 years after the end of the Civil War, social and economic legacies of institutionalized white supremacy still exist in our society. A fundamental effort at economic restitution has never yet been made. Our country has not paid its debt to a formerly enslaved people, nor have we addressed the deeper issues of their full economic integration into American society.

The moral challenge posed by Martin Luther King Jr. to the America people was this: having freed the slaves, what were they then freed *to*? The lack of a fundamental plan of economic repayment to a formerly enslaved population, and the denial of access to full economic recovery to generations that came after them, is at the root of many racial issues still existing to this day.

A pattern of greater poverty among black Americans remains unbroken, along with a pattern of less access to education and statistically less access to criminal justice. Those who see America today as a postracial society ignore certain underlying dynamics. "Blacks go to Harvard," they point out. "There are extremely wealthy black people now, and a black man became president!" Those comments are true, yet they are used like a mantra to gloss over continuing racial disparities in America. The fact that geniuses can make it in America doesn't in and of itself mean that full social justice exists in America. It doesn't mean that much work doesn't remain to be done.

Although it is true—and very much to be celebrated—that blacks have opportunities in America today unheard of even fifty years ago, those opportunities do not constitute full economic justice. One in five American children, 20 percent, live in poverty today, which ranks us as the country with the second-highest child poverty rate in the advanced world. Among black children, however, the poverty rate hovers at 40 percent. Being poor in America comes with lower-quality education, which leads to less economic opportunity; less economic opportunity often results in greater despair, which in turn produces greater dysfunction. These problems are not discrete and newly formed; they are the legacy of a situation that began in the 1600s and still plagues us today. Some instances of racism and white privilege within political, economic, and social policy have been drastically reduced over the last few decades. But in other arenas—particularly those related to criminal sentencing and incarceration—it could be argued that racism and white privilege have actually increased.

In 2013, the US Supreme Court took steps to gut the Voting Rights Act, making voter suppression—particularly among populations of color—a real and present danger to our democracy. This is unfortunately only one of the ways in which our commitment to racial justice has been dwindling rather than deepening over the last fifty years.

It is time for a new chapter in the history of racial reconciliation in America, involving a spiritual purification of the American heart, a deep national atonement, and willingness on the part of our country to make appropriate amends.

It's not as though racial tension finally erupted into violence on the streets of Ferguson, Missouri, in 2014 after a white police officer killed a black teenager. The situation continually erupts into violence in the hearts of black parents all over America each day, as they teach their children how to behave—particularly their sons—to avoid the unequal application of criminal justice in America. Most white Americans cannot imagine the layer of fear that runs through the psychic bloodstream of black Americans due to the killings of unarmed black men by police. And this problem isn't going to just magically disappear.

A politics of love is one in which we address the psychological and emotional wounds underlying our political realities and seek to heal them in meaningful ways. One such issue, when it comes to race in America, is our need for what is called in the Catholic Church a "purification of memory."

Until we fully appreciate the extent of a wrong done in the past, we cannot fully appreciate the ways in which we continue to repeat it. Educational and economic disparities in neighborhoods of color and racial disparities in criminal sentencing persist. And given that the current Department of Justice is seeking to roll back Obama-era efforts to improve these disparities, it is up to us, *we the people* of the United States, in order to form a more perfect union, to rise up and to speak out.

Racial healing is a journey through time. It would be a dishonor to our ancestors to minimize the struggles, sacrifices, and successes of past generations; but it would be similarly dishonoring to our descendants to fail to take the necessary steps, in our generation, to continue moving forward.

We know we have a race problem in America—manifested in the injustices of mass incarceration, the racial disparity in our criminal justice system, the lack of diversity in education and employment, instances of police brutality, rising white supremacy, and more. A greater sensitivity has emerged to the psychological and emotional nuances of white privilege, as well as its economic advantages. Yet the problem persists, poisoning the blood of our collective psyche. Just as an individual needs to identify and admit his or her character defects, so America has to identify our character defects as a nation. There is a strain of racist thought and feeling that has been with us from the beginning and is with us still. It is time for us to face it, atone for it, make amends for it, and end it. People can transform, and so can countries.

The question at the heart of our racial tension can also be found in immigration issues and other ethnic and religious prejudices: is the consciousness of America ready to evolve beyond the myth of Anglo-Saxon ownership? For many, the idea of a genuinely multiracial, multiethnic America represents the fulfillment of our national promise, while for others it represents a threat to some divine right granted to white people. And that is our psychic divide, the crooked place that must be made straight in our hearts. This country was established on the principle of *e pluribus unum*—"out of many, one"—yet the actualization of that principle remains a continuing work. And until we realize our spiritual oneness, the deeper work cannot be done.

Underneath the level of our bodies, we are spirits united in a holy oneness. Nothing short of that realization—not only grasped as an abstract concept, but experienced as an emotional reality carrying with it political imperatives—will save this country from our most self-destructive tendencies.

It was the task of a previous generation to abolish slavery, and it is the task of our generation to abolish racism. As a whole-person response to the problems of our time, a politics of love recognizes that both internal and external healing is necessary if we're to transform our country. Our sense of citizenship must include the purification of our hearts if we are to solve the problems of the world. In the words of Martin Luther

King Jr., "The desegregation of the American South is the externalization of the goal of the civil rights movement, but its ultimate goal is the establishment of the beloved community."

Dr. King knew that if all we do is address the externals of a problem, then the internal causes can still do damage. While the South has been desegregated, the American heart has not yet been totally purified of the scourge of racist thought and feeling. Just as a little bit of cancer can metastasize, the scourge of racism grows when left unchecked. And in many ways over the last few years, it has done just that. We have gone from a heady celebration of the successes of the civil rights movement in the 1960s to the injustices of mass incarceration, voter suppression, and white supremacists marching through the streets of Charlottesville, Virginia, in 2017.

We need to do more than feel bad about that. We need to *do* something.

A politics of love stands for more than incremental changes. It is a fundamental disruption, a revolutionary stance, and a proactive movement in the direction of a greater good. Whites can listen more to black Americans, and we should. Whites can do more to recognize the depths of white privilege, and we should. We can oppose voter suppression and disparities in our criminal justice system, and we should. We must do all those things. But we should also pay up.

# Time to Pay Up

I f you steal a lot of money from someone—and more than two hundred years of unpaid labor certainly amounts to a lot of it—then you owe them more than an apology. You owe them money.

After the South's defeat in the Civil War, the plan for Reconstruction included economic restitution to a formerly enslaved people. Yet many who worked hard to see such restitution occur were met with strong resistance by forces in both the North and South.

On January 16, 1865, Union general William Tecumseh Sherman promised forty acres and a mule to black farmers who had been enslaved. This compensation was extremely important because formerly enslaved agricultural workers had no way of entering an economy as free agents without the means to do so. Forty acres and a mule could provide the opportunity to establish themselves as free and economically independent citizens of the United States. A few former slaves were given that acreage, most of them only to see it returned to its former owners after the departure of federal troops from the South in 1877. From then until today, there has been no serious, concerted effort to repay the economic debt created by over two centuries of slavery.

In the 1990s, Bill Clinton suggested that we have a "national conversation about race." But it's difficult to have an authentic conversation when half of the people involved in the dialogue have over two hundred years of understandable rage to express. There are situations in life—and race in America is one of them—where talk without action does not heal a wound but only exacerbates it. Whites and blacks have a relationship in America, but it is an unequal one. One side owes something to the other, and until the debt is paid—or at the very least acknowledged—the relationship will remain unhealed.

By the twentieth century, the concept of reparations was widely recognized as a reasonable payment to a formerly wronged people. Germany has paid $89 billion in war reparations to Jewish organizations since World War II, and the United States should pay reparations for slavery. Germany could not undo the Holocaust, but reparations were part of its reconciliation with the Jews of Germany and the rest of Europe. America cannot undo hundreds of years of slavery either, but reparations can go far toward establishing a new frontier in racial reconciliation. Until then, each generation of Americans will continue to pass on to our children the toxicity of a psychological and economic debt.

In 1988, President Ronald Reagan signed the Civil Liberties Act to compensate more than a hundred thousand people of Japanese descent who were incarcerated in internment camps during World War II. The legislation included a formal apology and a payment of $20,000 to each surviving victim. Why should America not pay reparations to the descendants of slaves who were brought to America against their will, used as slaves to build the Southern economy into a huge economic force, and then freed into a culture of further violence perpetrated against them? The fact that slavery ended in 1865 doesn't mean the debt should be considered null and void. It certainly hasn't been nullified in the ethers.

The problem of racism is hardly behind us; when handled in one area, it has morphed into new symptoms in another. It is time for our generation to rise to the challenge and take a fundamental step closer to national atonement and amends.

While there is no one solution that solves every aspect of the problem, a plan of reparations would have significant psychic as well as economic effects. The United States should appoint a Reparations Commission comprising a council of black leaders from across the spectrum of American culture, academia, and politics. A payment of $100 billion—probably more—paid over a period of ten years, would then be disbursed to projects of economic and educational renewal in the black community as determined by the Reparations Council. This plan would be rendered as payment for a long overdue debt.

The argument, of course, will always be that we "can't afford it." Yet it is time to push back against such hypocrisy.

America will spend over $718 billion on defense this year alone. Over $2 trillion has been spent on the Iraq War, seen now to have been a massive foreign policy blunder. Two trillion dollars were given away in the 2017 tax cuts. Yet no one ever asked if we "could afford" such things. When it comes to paying reparations for slavery, on an emotional, psychological, and spiritual level we cannot afford not to. Until we do, the cycle of violence that began in the 1600s and continues to this day will continue to haunt our psyche and disrupt our good.

A politics of love is bold because love is bold. A politics of love does not just ask what's expedient; it asks what is right, and then seeks to do it.

# 7

# THE SOJOURNER AMONG US
## THE HOPE OF IMMIGRANTS

In 2017, traveling with friends to the Za'atari camp, a Syrian refugee camp in Jordan, I met three adorable little sisters so precious that I cried at having to leave them. Despite their parents' extraordinarily challenging circumstances, these beautiful, intelligent children were raised to be cheerful, disciplined, and friendly. They and the other children in the camp spent all day in class, at sports, even at a circus filled with clowns. Their parents made diligent efforts to make sure their lives were shielded from the harsher realities of their circumstances. Any of us would have been honored and delighted to have such well-adjusted children. Their joy and positivity were contagious.

Leaving the camp, I was silent in the car on the way back to our hotel. I wished everyone I knew in America could have spent the day as I had. I wished they could see the human reality behind the word *refugee*. I felt a painful juxtaposition between the character and refinement of the people I met at the Za'atari camp and the narrow-mindedness and closed-heartedness of America's current policies toward them.

Now, as I write this, people seeking asylum on the southern border of the United States are being scapegoated as criminals, their children deceitfully taken from their arms with no plan as to how they will be returned. In violation of American law, which mandates that almost anyone who sets foot in the United States has full constitutional protection here, and almost universally accepted human rights, these asylum seekers have been grossly denied fair protection. They are being prosecuted instead of welcomed, and their efforts to escape violence are being met by another kind of violence.

The traumatized cries of their separated children have become a rallying cry for the American conscience. A howl of outrage is being heard throughout America, not only because of the specific immigration policy of separating parents from children, but because of the moral descent that is represented by such a policy.

This is not the first time America's immigration policies have reflected the lower rather than higher angels of our nature. The Palmer Raids conducted in 1919 and 1920 during America's "First Red Scare" were responsible for over five hundred foreign citizens—mainly suspected radical leftists who were mostly Italian and Eastern European immigrants—being ripped from their homes, arrested, and illegally deported. Earlier, during the 1880s, a federal law called the Chinese Exclusion Act prohibited the immigration of all Chinese laborers. But we look back on such things in full awareness that they were wrong. Contemporary Americans are now facing something we have never had to face before: our government, caught red-handed in an act of transgression against one of our most treasured principles, responding with a brazen "Yeah, what of it?"

Scapegoating immigrants, particularly Mexicans, has been a primary fear tactic of our current president since the first day he announced his candidacy. Some took him seriously; some did not. Some saw the dangers of his rhetoric then; some did not. In fact, nothing is more dangerous than hatred harnessed for political purposes.

Scapegoating is a deliberate dehumanization technique. Americans had to see Africans as somehow less than fully human in order to enslave them. Americans had to see Native Americans as savages in order to acquiesce to the destruction of their culture. Germans had to see Jews as weeds in the garden of humanity in order to put them into death camps. Rwandan Hutus had to see Tutsis as animals; Chinese had to see students at Tiananmen Square as criminals; Croatians had to see Bosnian Muslims as enemies of the state, which is how

Turks had to see Armenians and Myanmar has to see Rohing-
yas today. Dehumanizing others has always been the required
first step in the commitment of history's collective atrocities.
Demonizing others brings out the demons in those who demonize.

When I was a child, my parents took my brother and sister
and me to many places around the world. My father was an
immigration lawyer, and I was taught at a very young age why
America mattered, what my grandparents had escaped from as
Jews living in Russia during the nineteenth century, and what
coming to America had meant to them. I learned early to appreciate the plight of the immigrant, the blessing of an American passport, and the value of a free society. I realized at an
early age that what makes America special is that people can
breathe free here. Not just that people can have *things*, but that
people can have freedom. That people can simply *be*.

I was around thirteen years old when our family visited Bu-
dapest, Hungary. Having been invaded by the Soviets in 1957,
that country was still living under Communist domination. A
young man had been our guide on the trip, and when he drove
us to the airport at the end of our time there I saw my father
surreptitiously hand him his business card and say in a very
low voice, "You get yourself out of here, and I'll take care of
you from there." I registered the tearful look of gratitude in the
eyes of that young man. Even as a child, I viscerally understood

in that moment what living under Soviet rule meant and what making it to America stood for.

My father himself was the son of poor immigrants. As a child, he was the only one in his family who could speak good English, and he was often asked to help his parents and their friends fill out immigration forms they couldn't read. My mother's father came to America alone when he was thirteen years old and sold bananas on the East Side of New York until he had raised enough money to return to Russia and get his next-younger brother; together they sold enough bananas to make the money to return and get their next-younger sibling; and on and on until all seven brothers and sisters and their mother had been brought over to America.

Through stories about the lives of strangers, and about the lives of my own family members, I was taught from an early age about the often desperate plight of the immigrant and the blazing hope that America held out to them. I remember my father explaining to me that at the time when his father grew up there, Jews in Russia were conscripted into the army for twenty-five years of service. Now, in our time, we read of people all over the world who endure situations more horrible and devastating to body and soul than we can imagine in order to make it to the shores of America, where life might be better for them and for their children. What makes their plight less devastating, or less worthy of human compassion, than that of our own ancestors?

# To Be Blessed, Be a Blessing

The plight of the modern refugee—the vast majority of whom are asylum seekers—is no different now than it ever was. What has changed is how anti-immigrant fervor has been weaponized in the modern era, taking a wrecking ball to something previously considered a point of pride for our country: that we're a nation of immigrants. At a time when we have a greater refugee crisis than at any point since World War II, with over 60 million people displaced or homeless worldwide—often, in fact, as a result of tragedies at least indirectly influenced by US foreign policy—America is closing its heart.

The United States has significant border security issues, and other immigration issues, that pose legitimate points for bipartisan problem-solving. But the bigger issue at the moment in this, as in so many other areas, is America's paramount need to return to our moral axis. Seeking asylum here is a statutory right established in the Refugee Act of 1980. While it's legitimate to discuss conservative versus progressive options regarding how we help a refugee fleeing humanitarian horrors, there should never be a question of whether or not we do.

Earlier this year, I visited Ellis Island. I was deeply moved not only by the building but by the museum exhibits included in a massive renovation of the island and its buildings in the 1980s. Visitors see a slice of history that is relevant to us all.

The building containing the Great Hall at Ellis Island opened on January 1, 1892, and from the time it opened until it closed in 1954, 12 million immigrants to the United States entered there. Four of them were my grandparents. Pictures at the exhibit show extraordinary images of immigrants from the late nineteenth through the mid-twentieth centuries—people from many countries, many backgrounds, all seeking a better life in America after having fled persecution, pogroms, and all forms of unspeakable hardship. It is impossible to look at the pictures at the Ellis Island Museum and not have a visceral understanding of what the history of immigration has meant to this country.

When I took the ferry back to the island of Manhattan, I saw a man playing music in Battery Park. He was an Asian man playing an exotic instrument I had never seen, a violin of some kind that emits the most gorgeous music. Across the sidewalk from him sat a woman in a headscarf, sitting on a bench and playing with her baby. Together with everyone else in the park that day, they formed a tableau of modern America. As moved as I was by the pictures in the museum, I was even more moved as I witnessed this man and woman, sitting opposite each other across the sidewalk, both having come from very different places but seeking the same possibility. He with his music and she with her baby, both were passing on to others the beauty of who they are.

The immigrant story of today contains no less richness, variety, contribution, creativity, and life pulsing at its most ordinary and beautiful than it did a hundred years ago. The immigrant is not our enemy. It is so important to remember this today, as immigrants are often viciously scapegoated. This is not the first time this has happened in America, and we must stand up against it now as other generations stood up against it in their time. The story of immigration in the United States has been ugly before. But we got through those earlier dark periods of mean-spiritedness in our history, and we will get through this one too.

On the way to Ellis Island our ferry stopped at the Statue of Liberty, where every visitor is reminded of the power of Lady Liberty's message. Her torch is held high, and it's not coming down. As long as she stands firm in our hearts, she will stand firm on that little island of hers. She keeps alive an eternal idea, created by God and a creed of our national identity. There are no strangers in God's universe, nor need there be any strangers in the family of man.

In 1883, Emma Lazarus wrote a sonnet titled "The New Colossus" to raise money for the construction of a pedestal for the Statue of Liberty. Millions of immigrants over the years have viewed the statue as they entered New York Harbor and knew that they had come home. Visiting Ellis Island today, one can practically feel the ghosts of the 12 million immigrants whose entrance to the United States was processed between the late nineteenth and the mid-twentieth centuries. Their hopes, their dreams, and their stories were not so unlike those of almost everyone seeking to enter America today.

Lazarus's poem, inscribed not only on the base of the statue but in the hearts of millions, is a reminder to all of us of one of our most treasured values. Yet its words, like the words in our founding documents, will lose moral force if we fail to embrace and protect them. A nation, like an individual, compromises its principles at the expense of its soul.

Poetry read quickly doesn't penetrate the soul. But poems such as this one, read slowly, savored and embraced, can change your entire view of being an American.

*Not like the brazen giant of Greek fame,*
*With conquering limbs astride from land to land;*
*Here at our sea-washed, sunset gates shall stand*
*A mighty woman with a torch, whose flame*
*Is the imprisoned lightning, and her name*
*Mother of Exiles. From her beacon-hand*
*Glows world-wide welcome; her mild eyes command*
*The air-bridged harbor that twin cities frame.*

*"Keep, ancient lands, your storied pomp!" cries she*
*With silent lips. "Give me your tired, your poor,*
*Your huddled masses yearning to breathe free,*
*The wretched refuse of your teeming shore.*
*Send these, the homeless, tempest-tost to me,*
*I lift my lamp beside the golden door!"*

Who do we resemble more today—the "brazen giant of Greek fame, with conquering limbs astride from land to land," or the "Mother of Exiles"? Do we really *want* to destroy the very notion of America as a nation of immigrants?

America has undoubtedly been blessed. But the blessings upon us are not due to some special dispensation from God; they're due to our having chosen to be a blessing to others. We set out to be a blessing, and as with all cause and effect, it was the blessing we gave to others that magnetized so much blessing to us. That is why it's so dangerous when we withdraw those blessings—as we do with policies like imposing a Muslim travel ban, separating children from their parents at the border, or enacting reckless environmental policies. We're not just messing with visible forces when we do that; we're messing with invisible forces too.

A question central to our current immigration drama is this: who we do we think America belongs to? How ironic that a people who stole this continent from Native Americans, who had lived here for thousands of years before we arrived, now turn around and claim some God-given right to ownership. It's like stealing a house and then proudly sending out a "We Moved" card to your friends.

Seeking asylum in America is not a scam, it is a statutory right. And immigrating to America is not a crime. The modern immigrant is chasing the same dream of a better life that lured the ancestors of every American who isn't descended from either slaves or Native Americans.

When I was a little girl, my father used to point out to us that the entire concept of national boundaries was created by man, not by God. He would have us look at an atlas, or a globe, in which the boundary lines weren't present, to see what the world looks like geographically from miles above. God didn't draw a line between France and Spain, or between the United States and Mexico. The whole idea of national boundaries is a man-made material category. National borders have a place in our material functioning. But they should be used to organize our societies, not to divide our hearts.

The deeper questions for a nation are the same as for an individual: did God put us on the earth to be brothers and sisters, or did He not? I was taught as a child that people are the same everywhere. The love of a mother for her child in Malawi is no different from the love of a mother for her child in Minnesota. No matter where we were born, no matter what our socioeconomic background, we are made of the same essence, the same intersection of the human and the divine.

We should reject any notion that while such sentiments might be lovely, they have nothing to do with politics. The humanity of all people should have *everything* to do with politics. I have never forgotten how my parents made us aware that here in the United States their parents and many millions like them had found refuge from lives of suffering and oppression. My siblings and I were not just taught to be grateful for that; we were taught to never forget where our family had come from, what a gift America had given to us, and the importance of that gift to so many people in the world. Too many Americans seem to take for granted a gift that did not just fall out of the sky; rather, our freedom was created through extraordinary struggle and sacrifice, meant to be passed from generation to generation. What we have received from our ancestors it is our moral responsibility to pass on to others.

What makes America great is that America is *good*. In both the Old and New Testaments, we are told to greet the stranger with respect and with an open heart. "Treat the sojourner as you do the native, for you were sojourners in the land of Egypt" (Leviticus 19:34). But many Americans today can't relate to the idea of being a refugee with nowhere to go, even though that was the plight of most of their own ancestors. We're allowing our national heart to harden, our moral compass to be driven off course, our critical thought processes to be jangled, and our minds to be propagandized by the notion that people who are no different from us are somehow our enemy.

Americans have an instinctive understanding that America matters and that it matters for a reason: to light the way for all humanity. But to lead the way, we must *be* the way. Hatred and bigotry and racism are not light; they are spiritual darkness, and it is that darkness out of which we must pull ourselves now. If our spiritual values matter at all, they must matter everywhere. And that includes in the arena of politics.

America's covenant with history is to always set our sights high, whether we are able to reach those heights or not. The push-pull relationship between the highs and lows of our national character is baked into the cake of America's historical narrative. We like to think, however, that as we evolve through time we move forward, with every generation adding to the formation of a "more perfect union." Today, dangerously and tragically, we are moving backwards in certain ways. The moment is perilous, though filled with miraculous possibility. We need a politics of love to put our nation back on its moral course.

# A Trumped-Up Crisis

Where some have harnessed fear for political purposes, it is time to harness love for political purposes. A politics of love not only says yes to what we do want; it is also capable of saying no to what we do not want. Where crowds have gathered to protest a Muslim ban or the forced separation of families, the spirit of the "Mother of Exiles" has expressed itself. And it will continue to do so. The better angels of our nature have often been silenced, but never forever. It is time for our generation to rise up as others have, to sing in our time the eternal song of a loving heart. Angels can sing only if we allow them to sing through us.

When someone says, "Yes, but what would *you* do about the immigration crisis?" remember this: although there are certainly reasonable changes that need to be made in our immigration policies, the idea that we have a *crisis* is simply a canard. Our border crisis is a made-up crisis, used to distract the most disadvantaged Americans from seeing who and what is really leeching their resources, who and what is really undercutting their power, and who and what is really stealing their democracy. In the words of Mayor Tony Martinez of McAllen, Texas, in the midst of the literally Trumped-up crisis at the border, "We were doing fine, quite frankly."

In fact, over the last decade, illegal immigration has been *going down*. There are no hordes of immigrants "infesting" us. And while no one wants violent criminals in our country, and all Americans want the violent gang MS-13 expunged both here *and* in El Salvador, the current anti-immigrant fervor has little or nothing to do with such matters. The actual rate of criminality among immigrants—even the undocumented—is lower, not higher, than the rate of criminality among our non-immigrant citizens. And the rate of their contributions, in fields ranging from the arts to science to academia, is at least as high. The deliberate attempt by some of our leaders to make Americans fear something so basic to our greatness in the *name* of our greatness will one day be seen as a dark, aberrational chapter in our nation's history.

The contributions of many of America's immigrant communities are among the highest of any subpopulation, whether measured culturally, academically, or economically. We have much more to fear from the domestic terrorism of anti-immigrant hordes than from anything immigrants are bringing into the country with them.

The hardening of the American heart is far more dangerous than the softening of our borders. Those who scapegoat immigrants, like demagogues throughout history, are demonizing others to increase their own power. Their lies, like all lies, have risen to prominence temporarily, but they will not stand.

It is only in devoting ourselves to the things this country stands for that we will reclaim our invulnerability to forces that would tear us down. It is not enough to be appalled by bigotry; we must rededicate ourselves to the idea of a nation in which bigotry has no place. I don't know any progressive who is arguing for open borders, but we *are* arguing for open hearts.

A politics of love is not just a sweet and gentle concept; it is a fierce and committed field of energy made of people who have awakened not only to the darkness in our midst but to the eternal light that casts it out. It is not enough that the Statue of Liberty holds the torch. Each of us must hold it in our hearts as well, and hold it high. Neither angels nor demons are a thing of the past. They are present in the choices we make today: whether to stand for love . . . or not.

# 8

# WAR AND PEACE
## FIGHTING THE PROFITS OF WAR

A politics of love is neither unsophisticated nor naive about the dangers of the world; it acknowledges the need for military preparedness. But in the world as it is today, we need to know as much about how to wage peace as how to wage war.

The US military deserves the utmost respect from every American. Those who serve display not only advanced expertise but also advanced devotion: a willingness to sacrifice their lives in service to their country. Any criticism of US military policy is not a criticism of the military itself, but of the civilian leadership that controls it.

Our military should be like the best surgeon in the world. Of *course* we want to have the very finest surgeon available if we need surgery. But any sane person tries to avoid surgery if possible. We should go to war only because we *need* to go to war. Our defense establishment should not be a self-perpetuating war machine.

Yet that is basically what has happened over the last few decades, as we have fallen into a continuing pattern of war that few even dare to question. Most Americans couldn't tell you which countries we're engaged with militarily at this point. After 9/11, through the Defense Authorization Act, Congress gave the president unprecedented authorization to do whatever he wants in the name of fighting terrorism (decidedly against the "advise and consent" clause of the Constitution), basically giving the executive branch of our government carte blanche over military authority. All we can do is pray that they're getting it right.

The US Constitution made the president commander-in-chief of the US armed forces in order to guarantee civilian control of our military. This is how the Founders protected a democratically elected government from being overturned by a military coup. But while it's important that the military work at the behest of the president, it's also important for us to remember that the president and Congress work at the behest of *us*. This is one more area where financial corruption, so endemic to our current politics, has put advocacy for corporate profits—in this case, military defense contractors—before advocacy for the health and well-being of the American people.

No American would argue against protecting our homeland. But enemy threats today do not arrive only via land, air, or sea; they also arrive over the internet. Terrorists don't trade in warships, bombers, or submarines, but in pathological ideas and malevolent cyberwar. And they're not always foreign fighters either; they are just as likely to have been born and raised right here. America today is like the British Red Coats during the Revolutionary War—standing abreast in a straight line waiting for someone to yell "Fire!" while American colonists were hiding behind trees like the early guerrilla fighters that they were. Our entire notion of national security is like something out of another century.

That is why in this area, as in so many others, we will adequately address our challenges only if we are willing to rethink them. We will be able to keep our nation safe in the years ahead only if we think differently about war, and differently about peace. In the words of Franklin D. Roosevelt, "We must do more than end war. We must end the beginnings of all wars."

Traditional warfare addresses external realities, seeking to suppress or eradicate malignant symptoms. But with society as well as with the body, we ultimately cannot just treat symptoms; we need to treat their cause. We can't just fight the symptoms of hate; we must cultivate the love in the presence of which hate does not grow. Most of our problems are opportunistic infections, none of which would have gained such power had our societal immune cells been healthier. That is why cultivating justice and brotherhood is more than just a "nice" thing to do; by cutting off its oxygen, the politics of love is the most sophisticated response to evil. This century demands a different mental framework through which to view the entire notion of security. In today's world, no amount or means of brute force can provide an absolute guarantee of our safety.

We should see the soul force of peace-building, then, as central to our efforts to create a peaceful world. Our conversation around national security rarely names the goal of creating peace at all, and that is where our modern political establishment most fails us. Peace is not the absence of war; war is the absence of peace. Preparing for and waging war—while it might fend off some enemies at times (while often creating new ones as well)—is not the most potent tool for peace creation.

# Profits of War

Our current national security strategy is all about war and very little about peace. If we really wanted peace in the world, then we would strive for peace. But a quick look at America's national security budget makes it obvious that peace is not our direct goal. Peace is just something we sort of hope we'll back into.

Our Defense Department now functions in a role of dual advocacy, both for America's security interests and also for the economic interests that accrue to military defense contracts. Where the interests collide, at present the defense industry tends to win out. A case in point is America's current relationship with Saudi Arabia. For the sake of over a billion dollars in arms contracts, the United States is providing arms to the kingdom in a war that has led to the starvation of tens of thousands. Also, Boeing has signed a $500 million contract to provide technical support. Even the brutal murder of a Saudi journalist, a legal permanent resident of the United States, wasn't enough to tear us away. The State Department issued a statement saying it's possible for us to have "strategic partnerships" with people who do not share our values. Which is to say that it's okay for us to have no values at all.

Supporting our military is very different from supporting

the multibillion-dollar behemoth of military contractors that make up America's current war machine. Too often today young people die on battlefields so that old people can get rich selling armaments. It's not enough to have private morals if we, as citizens, are willing to acquiesce to the complete surrender of our public ones.

It was the Republican president Dwight Eisenhower—the supreme Allied commander during World War II—who, in his farewell address to the nation, warned us of what he called the "military-industrial complex." This is the enduring financial and political alliance that makes war such big business— now on the scale of a $718 billion annual US defense budget. Today our defense budget outstrips those of China, Russia, the United Kingdom, France, Japan, Saudi Arabia, and India combined.

Before World War II, the United States had no standing army; while no one would argue that we don't need one in the present age, neither should we deny the risk that comes with making war into such big business. Too often, weapons are not manufactured to help fight wars so much as wars are manufactured to help sell weapons. If defense manufacturers stand to make billions of dollars off the machinery of war, there will always be more and more political pressure to provide theaters in which to use it.

In less than one hundred years America has gone from

military power "as needed" to military power as big business, with the attendant false glamorization that all militarized societies proffer. All this has led to subtle and not-so-subtle ways in which Americans have begun to think differently about war. It is no longer something we do only when we have to; it has become something that is sort of just "always there." When there was a draft, war was never just "over there." Without a draft, it's far too easy for all of us to simply look away. This is not an argument for the reinstatement of the draft, but it is an argument for the reawakening of the American mind.

# Speak Softly and Carry a Big Stick

When I was a child, as we watched images of military parades in the former Soviet Union on TV, we were taught that we didn't *do* things like that in America. And we were proud of it. When Dwight Eisenhower was the supreme commander of all Allied forces, he obviously wore military clothes, but as president, he just as proudly wore civilian clothes. Not just the symbolism of these differences but the energy they carry can determine how a society perceives itself. We are not a military society, and we don't want to become one.

President Theodore Roosevelt described his foreign policy this way: "Speak softly and carry a big stick." No one in the world doubts how powerful our military is. But the military misadventures of the last half century have garnered us neither greater respect nor friendship nor affection. Quite the opposite: millions around the world, having witnessed American involvement in wars such as those in Vietnam and Iraq, see no reason to believe that America is always a beacon of democracy or that the US military is effective at solving every problem.

This is not a conundrum for politicians alone to handle; it is an issue for all of us to wake up to. It's said that war is too important to be left to the generals, but it's also too important to be left to the politicians. Our political establishment is enamored of the power of brute force, and undervalues the power of soul force. We need to adopt a new political mind-set if we are to deliver to our children and our children's children any semblance of a peaceful world.

Only those who are either ignorant of history or willfully blind to it can deny the role of widespread human despair, economic hardship, and lack of education in fostering eruptions of violence around the world. Only when we consciously and willingly address those issues in a meaningful way will we be paving the way to a sustainable peace on earth. We can't just go around fighting violence all the time; we must learn how to cultivate peace.

At present, the resources we spend on building true foundations of peace—diplomacy, support for democratic institutions, expansion of economic opportunities for women, providing educational opportunities for children, and ameliorating human suffering—are minuscule compared to what we spend on defense.

An example of our war-for-profit mentality is the following. The US Air Force has recently ordered one hundred B-21 raiders at a cost of over $550 million each, for a total price tag of $55 billion. Each of these stealth bombers carries both conventional and thermonuclear weapons, begging the question: are we planning to drop one hundred thermonuclear bombs? Of course not. But it's relevant to ask, because once even four or five of those start dropping, it's over for all of us. It's difficult emotionally to even *think* about a prospect like nuclear war. Yet that is exactly where America needs a revolution in consciousness: our willingness to think about some very serious things.

It is our denial, our avoidance of such painful topics, that is most dangerous to us now. We have gone from being a country with a vital ban-the-bomb movement—the Nuclear Test Ban Treaty of 1963 was a really, really big deal—to one where the average citizen has been lulled to sleep, where the very subject seems so complicated, so difficult, that many of us have *just left it to other people to think about.* Yet the people we've left to think about it are the same ones ordering those B-21 raiders! That is why we are where we are today. You simply can't outsource your thinking, your conscience, or your heart.

Even the smallest nuclear bomb that exists today, if it were to be detonated in a major city, would kill hundreds of thousands, if not millions, of people. This is not a technological issue; it is not even a military issue. It is a human issue.

For the $550 million we are spending on just one B-21 raider, we could ameliorate the human suffering of billions of people around the world. That would be the moral thing to do. That would be the loving thing to do. And that would be the smart thing to do.

To whom in America do we turn for moral guidance in handling issues of war and peace? Theoretically, that would be our president and Congress. Yet the moral judgment of our politicians is far too often sacrificed at the altar of financial and political corruption.

As an example, the defense authorization bill approving President George W. Bush's invasion of Iraq was based on the political considerations of that moment more than on deep and sober analysis of US intelligence. In fact, most members of Congress apparently did not read the full analysis made available only to them in classified reports. That would have meant walking down the hall.

The US military establishment has become a gargantuan enterprise with seemingly no moral oversight whatsoever. No religious, spiritual, or philosophical voices are publicly asked to contribute in any meaningful way to a political topic that could determine whether humanity lives or dies. Yet if whether we kill each other is not a question for moral consideration, I don't know what is.

Not only are we dealing with the reality of nuclear bombs now, we're dealing with a plethora of them, and some are not in the hands of responsible people. The idea that we can deal with the issue only through an ever-escalating arms race—even to the point, being currently discussed, of putting nuclear bombs in outer space—is not responsible. It is insane.

A politics of love expands the political conversation by expanding its human dimension. Institutions do not change quickly, but people's attitudes can, and Americans are good at doing that. One of the greatest dangers posed by the breakdown of our democracy, as evidenced by the disconnect between the consciousness of our people and the actions of our government, is the threat this poses to our national security. People are evolving in one direction and our government is evolving in another. People are clamoring for peace; too often our politicians are clamoring for war. If we the people don't inject some higher consciousness into the conversation soon, then God help us all.

A politics of love takes an integrative approach to political issues. The same holistic paradigm that has transformed our view of physical health can be applied to our societal health. We know better than to think that we can avoid taking responsibility for our heath and not expect to get sick. We know better than to think that we can avoid paying attention to our nutrition, exercise, and lifestyle and then simply suppress or eradicate any symptoms of sickness that may arise. We realize that we must cultivate our health if we want to be healthy, not simply fight sickness when it appears.

We should apply that same logic to issues of war and peace. We should know better than to think that we can avoid taking responsibility for peace and not expect war. Active peace-building measures reinforce the social health of our planet the way good nutrition and exercise reinforce the physical health of our bodies.

Currently, not only are more and more resources being added to our defense budget, but more and more resources are being withdrawn from actual peace-building. Since the beginning of 2017, while building up our military, our president has routinely attempted to strip our government of programs that provide humanitarian aid and support diplomacy, education, campaigns to eliminate violence against women, refugee assistance, mediation, postconflict and restorative justice, democracy-building, and other critical peace-building measures.

What would it look like for a politics of love to infuse the workings of the US government? Among other things, we should foster a far more equal working partnership between the Defense Department and the State Department to handle international security needs. James Mattis, the former secretary of defense, said that if we didn't fund the State Department fully, then he would need to order more ammunition. We should establish a US Department of Peace to identify and foster domestic peace-creating projects in the United States; outbreaks of violence here are as horrifying as those anywhere else in the world. We could make peace-creation central to all domestic and international policy, not just in word but in deed.

While some say it's naive to believe that massively realigning resources toward helping people thrive—by leading efforts to eradicate global poverty, support democratic institutions, and expand economic and educational opportunities—is central to creating peace in the twenty-first century, we need to unabashedly insist that it's naive to assume humanity will even survive the twenty-first century if we do not.

A more loving life is a *smarter* life—smarter for our health and for the health of our planet. When it comes to international relations, if someone asks, "What's love got to do with it?" the answer is "Everything." In study after study, the success rate of "soft powers" at dissolving international conflicts has proved greater than that of military might. Love is not a less sophisticated worldview; it is a *more* sophisticated worldview. There's nothing sophisticated at all about viewing security only in terms of bombs on land or sea, when the first bombs that go off are inside a person's heart.

Again, in the words of President Dwight D. Eisenhower, a Republican:

> *Every gun that is made, every warship launched, every rocket fired signifies, in the final sense, a theft from those who hunger and are not fed, those who are cold and are not clothed.*
>
> *This world in arms is not spending money alone. It is spending the sweat of its laborers, the genius of its scientists, the hopes of its children. . . .*

*This is not a way of life at all, in any true sense. Under the cloud of threatening war, it is humanity hanging from a cross of iron.*\*

We are hanging on a cross of iron right now. And this is not just corrupt; it is dangerous for us all. Large groups of desperate people anywhere in the world should be seen as a national security risk, as desperate people do desperate things. The problem isn't just that some people hate us; it's also that a lot of people who never really hated us just don't like us anymore either. They too often see us not as a beacon of democracy, but as a bullying and imperialistic power. And that makes them far more vulnerable to ideological capture by genuinely psychotic forces.

After World War I, the economic devastation of the defeated German nation was a primary factor in the rise of Hitler. After World War II, we did not make the same mistake, but rather passed the Marshall Plan to help all of Europe rebuild. The best way to create a more peaceful world is to treat people with greater compassion. Our task is to replace a politics of fear with a politics of love. Love is a wiser, more evolved, and more powerful modus operandi than fear, if our goal is to bequeath a habitable world to our children and our children's children.

---

\* Dwight D. Eisenhower, "The Chance for Peace," speech delivered April 16, 1953, Washington, DC

# Waging Peace

As children of God, peace is our natural state of being. It is our moral responsibility to cultivate the conditions in which our natural state of being can thrive.

Every cause has an effect, and there is no way to obstruct the ultimate consequences of our actions. That is why war waged for any purpose other than absolute necessity is a danger not only to the victims of its perpetrators but to those who perpetrate it as well. The tragic mistake that was the invasion of Iraq, for instance, should arouse within us more than a collective "Oops." It should arouse within us the deepest realization of the horrors we unleashed both for ourselves and others, and a sincere attitude of atonement before God.

The women of America are key to challenging the insanity of America's war habit. If nothing else, we should be awakened by the fact that more women and children die in wars than do male combatants. We should unabashedly stand up to militarism, viewing this stance as simply one more way of dismantling the patriarchy. Feminine values like nurturing children and caring for the home are not just peripheral issues; they are the keys to peace on earth.

If Americans are to adequately deal with terrorism, we need to look deep into our own hearts and minds. A trigger-happy propensity for war should give way to a taste for wisdom, maturity, and reflection. The false power of the tough cowboy should dissolve now, giving way to the genuine power of wisdom. We should reach not only for a rich society but for a good society, both in how we behave at home and in how we express ourselves abroad.

According to research done by the Friends Committee on National Legislation, "The world spends just $1 on conflict prevention for every $1,885 it spends on military budgets. In the US, less than 2 percent of income tax goes to civilian foreign affairs agencies; while, 39 percent goes to the military. And though taxpayers provide almost $1 billion per year for military academies, they pay only about $40 million for the United States Institute of Peace—the only US agency dedicated to conflict prevention and peace-building." All this despite the fact that investing early to prevent conflicts from escalating into violent crises is, on average, sixty times more cost-effective than intervening after violence erupts.

The problem does not lie with our military; the problem lies with our politics. And the problem lies with us.

We the people must become deeper thinkers now. No think tank's research or government commission's findings can substitute for the power of personal reflection and citizen engagement. A corrupt government will do what we allow it to do. We need to say things that a lot of politicians are not going to say, and insist that they do some things that they otherwise will not do.

We need to look at some difficult facts of American history over the last sixty years. The United States, for instance, through the invasion of Iraq, was the biggest factor in the formation of ISIS. Could we not take a moment away from our popular amusements to seriously reflect on the suffering caused by that immoral, illegal invasion? And should we feel no remorse? The only person who feels no remorse, who expresses no regret, is a sociopath. An entire country failing to do so is no less pathological.

You don't get to irresponsibly cause thousands upon thousands of tragic deaths and then just say, "Oops." Nor should we allow ourselves, or anyone else, to perpetuate the canard that "Oh well, they acted on the best information they had at the time." Actually, no, they didn't. The pretext for the Iraq war was a "major intelligence failure," according to the Bush administration's own report, and they knew exactly what they were doing at the time by misleading Congress and the world. We invaded a country that had nothing to do with 9/11, that was actually serving as a buffer between us and Iran, and whose leader was a secularist who kept Al Qaeda at bay; and with no serious plan for rebuilding a city that we ourselves destroyed. None of those factors can be ignored by a conscious person, or a conscious country. Even if Iraq had had weapons of mass destruction, we do business with countries that have weapons of mass destruction each and every day. Even though Saddam Hussein was a horrible murderer who terrorized his people and killed many innocents, we routinely do business with governments that have done the same. Is anyone thinking the Chinese arrived in Tibet with candy? How easily we, the American people, acquiesced to something so wrong.

In a nation's life as well as an individual's, invisible forces of healing are released when we admit the exact nature of our wrongs and atone for them in our hearts. Only then can we pave the way to new beginnings.

America will not move forward into a new era of greatness unless we atone for the militaristic madness that has gripped our country in the years since World War II. We fought that war because we needed to. We've fought at least a couple of wars since then for one reason only: because someone wanted to. Dealing with America's militarism—not just in the leaders who led us into wars that in retrospect we can see to have been huge mistakes, but also in us, that we acquiesced so easily to them at times—is essential to disrupting the dangerous patterns that now threaten our future. Militarism, like racism, has become an American character defect. We must soberly realize this, humble ourselves before God, pray for forgiveness, and seek fundamental change.

Too many times, as a nation, we have chosen the ways of

war over the ways of peace, the ways of mean-spiritedness over the ways of compassion, the ways of separation over the ways of unity, and the accumulation of money over the accumulation of good. What we need more than anything now is to return to the wisdom in our hearts.

In the words of President John F. Kennedy, "This country cannot afford to be materially rich and spiritually poor." People heard those words when he uttered them, and we need to hear them today.

At times such as these, understanding the powers of the spirit is as important as understanding the powers of the world. The meek shall inherit the earth because, in the end, they are stronger. To be secure, we need to ask deeper questions than "What should we do?" We need to ask, "Who should we be?" And "Who should we be to each other?"

After the *Charlie Hebdo* tragedy in Paris in 2015, where twelve French journalists were killed by Islamist terrorists, a rally of two million people on the streets of Paris provided a beautiful show of solidarity. Such solidarity is what we need now, not just as a *reaction* to tragedies, but as a way of preventing them in the first place. When men, women, and children feel like they belong to something, feel that they are part of something, feel that they stand for something meaningful— that *is* the answer. It is the key to peace abroad, and it is the key to peace at home. What could be a more horrific irony than that jihadists say they feel a sense of *community*? The only thing more powerful than a brotherhood of hate is a brotherhood of love.

A "brotherhood of love" is not just a metaphor, and "the better angels of our nature" is not just a symbol. Both represent a matrix of choices made moment by moment as to how we will behave, how we will treat each other, and how we will choose to live our lives. They also represent the existential challenge now facing humanity: will we or will we not grow into the people we need to be now—to endure the times in which we live, navigate the times in which we live, and transform the times in which we live?

As any expert will tell you, there is no way to track down and stop everyone who has ever been radicalized. The force now tapping into the darkest corners of the human psyche, both here and abroad, will be defeated only from the most light-filled corners of the human heart.

# When the Bottom Line Is People

For years, when politicians spoke of America's "vital national interests," I assumed they meant peace, the cultivation of our democratic values, and genuine security. Little did I know how often they had in mind the care and protection of American and multinational corporate interests.

Our vital national interests do not lie in protecting Lockheed Martin, Halliburton, Boeing, and Exxon. That they and companies like them provide thousands of jobs is true, the importance of which is not to be minimized. But they are also companies that could be transformed through values of corporate responsibility to serve a peacetime rather than a war economy, and a green rather than an oil-based economy. In issues ranging from war to climate change, what such corporations do now, in too many cases, not only does not serve our vital national interests but actually works against them.

Our vital national interests lie in protecting the 3.1 million children who die from hunger-related preventable causes each year, the 71 percent of the world's population who live on less than $10 a day, and the nearly one billion people who live on less than $1.90 a day. It is the humanitarian aid workers, diplomats, and peace-builders who most serve our vital national interests. The amelioration of unnecessary human suffering, both here and around the world, should be the bottom line of all US policy.

It is not the radicalism of hate that is our biggest danger today; our biggest danger is that we lack the radicalism of love. That is the revolution now to be waged: a change in our thoughts, along with a change in our behavior, along with change in our institutions, along with a change in our votes, that will lead in time to a change in our world.

Any conversation less radical than that simply plays into the hands of those who despise us. We have the power to override the heinous efforts of those who terrorize, to overrule them and nullify their malevolence. But it cannot be done with mere military might.

What we need now is our spiritual might. The real war is not without, but within: between ego-based fear and spirit-based love. That is the contest that matters the most, and it rages constantly inside our heads. Will we choose brute force or soul force to provide for our security? As long as we the people are not answering that for ourselves, there will always be others seeking to provide the answers for us. Whether we let them do so will determine the fate of our precious world.

# 9

# TO BEGIN AGAIN
## THE CHOICE BEFORE US

People think politics is so ugly, and part of it is. But there is something else there too, when we allow it to unfold—something noble and meaningful and good. As someone who has been speaking to audiences regularly for thirty-five years, I have seen something wonderful happen when people sit together in a room and consider the most significant questions about their common existence.

My father was a lawyer, and he always said that you should speak to the smartest person on the jury. I have had the good fortune in my career to see people at their best—not necessarily when they were at their happiest, but when they were at their deepest and most real. Whether counseling a single person or a couple or talking to a large audience, I have been with people in that place—everyone knows it, we've all been there—where life is serious and hushed and true, even when painful. We should participate in politics with the same level of consciousness we bring to intimate love and therapy, parenting, and all of our most important and meaningful pursuits. We should bring all of ourselves to politics. We should bring our hearts and minds and deepest dedication to something bigger than ourselves. Politics is very, very serious business in a country as big and powerful as ours; when we get it right, it can be a beautiful thing, but when we get it wrong, it can be a terrible thing. And we are all responsible for that. With every election, with every campaign, we are deciding something extremely important. We are deciding what is possibly the fate of millions, the fate of the earth, even perhaps the fate of humanity. If that is not a sacred charge, I cannot imagine what is.

Americans are a good and decent people, no different from people anywhere else. Although fear and bigotry have been harnessed for political purposes, we have love and decency we can harness too. But first we must find and harness them within ourselves. We all have to look at ourselves and check our judgments at the door. A nonviolent revolution begins with facing, and surrendering, the violence within ourselves.

What's going to save this country is a massive revival of spirit among the American people.

I've seen how the energy in a room can change profoundly when we drop into our hearts for a meaningful, sober, sincere conversation about things that matter most. The political atmosphere shifts when the spiritual atmosphere shifts, and that is as true among the masses as it is in a small room. I have witnessed and experienced what happens when love has joined two people's hearts together. I have also witnessed and experienced what happens when love has joined the hearts of two thousand.

That is the kind of social movement that America needs now; not a community of hate but a community of love. All the great social justice movements in America's history have been born out of religious and spiritual communities, because that is who takes love most seriously. We should address social, political, and economic issues from the highest level of consciousness. For if you know how to heal one heart, then you're the one who knows how to heal the world.

# A Renewing of the Mind

Those who recognize the effects of the invisible realm are not antiestablishment; they are forming what is in essence a new establishment, a much-needed correction to the overly materialized focus of the twentieth century. The significance of the founding of the United States was itself metaphysical: the declaration of a radical new possibility for the human race, a philosophical as much as a political revolution to overthrow the chains that bind. Never yet fully attained or embodied, the American Dream remains the light upon our path—our mission to ensure that all citizens, regardless of race, creed, or religion, be allowed the material means of self-actualization. This radical commitment to human possibility must be thrown down like a gauntlet in the face of oppression, in any form, at any time, and by every generation. The last thing we need to do is whine about the fact that other generations didn't complete the task; it is every generation's job to carry it forward, to build on the success of those who came before, and to disrupt any patterns of failure we've inherited. We need to emotionally recommit ourselves to the sacred charge we've been handed, not only for ourselves but for all the world.

Strong forces, both in the mind and in the world, would pull us down into the mire of despair. But equally strong, even stronger forces compel us to rise up. That is true for us as individuals, and true for us as a country. We must clean up the past and make way for new beginnings.

Jim Forbes, the former senior minister at Riverside Church in New York and a friend and mentor, once pointed out to me that the "end days" are not just times of "wars and rumors of war"—they are also times of "signs and wonders." If these are the end times, they are also wondrous times. And perhaps what is ending is what needs to end, so something miraculous can now be born. For where there is love, there are always miracles. It is ours to choose, and the time to choose is now. The choice lies in what we choose to express, what we choose to foster, what we choose to embrace, and what we choose to commit to.

It is time to make the choice for love.

Love is not passive; it is active in the world. And there is much to be done. In the words of Dr. King, "Those who love peace must learn to organize as effectively as those who love war. . . . When evil men plot, good men must plan. When evil men burn and bomb, good men must build and bind. When evil men shout ugly words of hatred, good men must commit themselves to the glories of love."

Ah yes, to commit ourselves to the glories of love. We're a nation that has become more concerned with being rich than with being good, more concerned with getting more than with being more, more concerned with what happens on the outside than with what happens on the inside. And it is killing us. Human beings were created to love each other, not to hate each other; we were created as brothers and sisters, not as enemies; and we were created to be reverent, not to be too cool to care.

We must resist the temptation to intellectual and emotional shallowness that defines our popular culture today. We need to disavow the chronic silliness that has us playing at life like children rather than tending to life as genuine, powerful, responsible men and women. We need reverence toward each other, toward the children of the world, and toward the planet itself. We need reconciliation with the God of our understanding, and radical forgiveness toward each other. We need to look at ourselves and ask how we can do better, devote ourselves to our country and to our children's children, to rise up from the ashes of our self-preoccupation. We need desperately to evolve from "me" to "we." Only then will our country rise—when we rise first.

Democracy gives us rights, but it also gives us responsibilities, not just to receive the blessings of liberty but to tend to them in our time and bequeath them to our children. This is not a job for someone else. It's a job for each of us. We the people are the only true guardians of democracy. We have a much greater purpose on earth than to just get what we want.

That has always been America's greatness: that we stood for something higher than ourselves and strove for something higher than ourselves. Until we retrieve that greatness, we will continue to go down. But as soon as we do retrieve it, we will miraculously rise up again. For on the level of spirit we have wings.

# The Power of Love

One evening I was sitting in a hotel room in Charlottesville, Virginia, having given a talk at a church there earlier in the day. I noticed that the Mr. Rogers movie *Won't You Be My Neighbor?* was available on the room's TV, and having heard several people mention it, I turned it on. By the end of the movie, I was sitting on the edge of my bed with tears flowing down my cheeks. Here, in a city that had been beset by an incident of American hate, I'd seen a movie that was a testament to American love.

Interestingly enough, I then turned on the local news—which I used to skip over when I went to a town until I realized that that's where you see some of the best news ever: the good news! It's where you see what real people do to make their lives and their communities better, from volunteer-run hunger programs (there should not be hunger in America!) to small business expos (a teenage girl selling earrings she had made, saying, "I do this because I didn't want to always be asking my mom for money") and festivals at public schools (these kids are so earnest I can't stand it, it's so beautiful). So many of the things that used to seem corny now seem so radical, so relevant: people simply loving each other, trying to do the right thing. We've so strayed from the basics—we all know we have—and we're all dying to get back to them. The small pleasures of life turn out to be the best ones. Small, random acts of kindness really do occur everywhere; we need to take all that love now and turn it into power.

We shouldn't underestimate the dangers of this moment, but neither should we underestimate the love in our hearts that can guide us through it. Mahatma Gandhi said that the real leader of the Indian independence movement was "the small still voice within." The small still voice within will lead our generation too, for it hasn't gone away. It is an aspect of human consciousness. It is an eternal internal guidance system. Each of us has a job to do, a unique part to play in the repairing of our world, and we can be internally guided as to what part is ours to play.

It isn't always easy for us to know what to do, but it wasn't easy for our ancestors either. The abolitionists, the suffragettes, the civil rights workers—they too were traumatized by their circumstances and stressed by the enormity of the challenges before them. But they rose to the occasion, and so must we. They heard the call and responded to it. They did their part; now it's time for us to do ours. The calling of the heart that called to them is now calling to you and me.

Minimizing the importance of the inner life is a legacy of a time now passing. At a time when the stresses on our planet— from climate change to out-of-control machineries of war—

are so rampant, nothing is more realistic than to seek answers from within.

Consider spending five minutes every day sitting with your eyes closed, sending love from your heart to everyone in your country, and then extending that love to every sentient being in the world. Such meditative practice opens the mind to new dimensions of problem-solving as new synapses, new insights, new connections arise automatically. Our biggest failure is to limit our imaginations to twentieth-century prejudices, surrendering to the insidious illusion that there's a limit to what's possible. Where there is love, possibilities are endless. But they do not emerge from the world as we know it; they emerge from a place that lies beyond our normal waking consciousness.

At a certain time, abolishing slavery in America would not have been seen as a reasonable proposition. Gaining women the right to vote would not have been seen as a reasonable proposition. Ending segregation would not have been seen as a reasonable proposition. When it comes to disrupting what appears like an intractable status quo, reason alone isn't our guiding light. The good, the true, and the beautiful emerge from a quantum realm of infinite possibility, when love and intention and commitment and devotion override all other factors.

It is not just our plans but also our imaginations that will summon the next great chapter of our history. It is not our reason but our hearts that will take us to the Promised Land. It isn't an angry no to those who don't know better, but rather a tender yes to the possibilities for a different kind of future that will open the door to the world we want.

How do we make love our agenda? By making it everything. Our generational problem, more than anything else, is our lack of full devotion. The miracle that will take us forward now is a 100 percent commitment to being who we need to be now, and doing what we need to do. We must not give in to the demonic chatter that life is lived for any other purpose than our capacity to love each other.

Teilhard de Chardin's amazing words—"someday, after mastering the winds, the waves, the tides, and gravity, we shall harness for God the energies of love"—should no longer be seen as a distant aspiration for some mythic future. What we are talking about now is our today and tomorrow. We will discover the fire of love, or we will be destroyed by the fires of fear.

Something is rising up from the depths today, centered not in any one geographical area, ethnic identity, or national identity. It's the evolutionary lure of a sustainable future, calling us to remember who we really are and inviting us to rise up from the past. It is a hunger felt among all the people of the world. We are stirred to live our lives in a different way; to align ourselves with something truer and deeper than mere bricks and mortar or dollars and cents. This stirring brings with it a deeper reverence, for earth and sky, and for each other. If we truly want a different world, we must be willing to think in a different way and live in a different way than we do now.

Our children do not deserve to be burdened by the insidious delay tactic of passing on to them the work that is ours to do. This is our time. The mess is ours to deal with, the challenge is ours to meet, and the miracle is ours to claim.

Consciously abandoning holiness, we have subconsciously become prey to all that is not holy. We must rid ourselves of darkness now, by turning on the light of the higher mind. Its power alone can break the chains that bind us to a limited and unjust world. It gives us the strength to imagine, to work for, and to summon a more beautiful world.

The call that should beckon us is not the call of our pocketbooks but the call of our hearts—an ancient melody that lies in all of us and can never be totally forgotten. Let us awaken to the call of love reborn, hope restored, and life renewed. We can—and in fact we have no other choice. Death awaits us if we do not choose life.

Human beings can descend, but we can rise back up. We can choose wrongly, but we can choose again. Humanity has come to a fork in the road, and each of us is responsible for choosing which way we go now. There is a way marked Love and there is a way marked Fear, each path leading to more of the same.

Our powerlessness is feigned. We are not powerless at all. We are simply in the habit of disengaging from the things that matter most. We can change that. We are waiting for nothing but our own true selves, our commitment, our conviction, and our choice to choose again. Our national salvation begins when we consider the possibility that there might be another way. There is no reason, no wisdom, in holding on to past, unworkable ways. Moreover, there is no survivable future there.

In our finest hours, America has stood for what humanity at our best aspires to be. We have sometimes succeeded and sometimes failed, but today, in our time, it is ours to decide our path as we move forward. Lady Liberty's torch is in our hands, but only we can determine whether it burns within our hearts. Either we will allow it to illumine our understanding, or consciously or unconsciously we will burn down the house.

The mass of humanity is crying out for another way, and that way will be found. All walls will fall away that block us from our destiny. The only questions are, How much suffering will have to occur before that happens, and Will America be a leader in finding a new way—or one of the greatest victims to the old? Shall we pave the way to humanity's higher purpose, in line with our historical mission, or shall we continue our current stumble into the depths of an irredeemable fall? This is not a rhetorical question. It is quite a literal one, and it cannot be answered by anyone but ourselves.

The day has come for an American reckoning. This is not the time to close our eyes, but to open them to the light within. It is a time of atonement, a time of replanting, and a time of deliverance. Or not; the choice is ours. In honor of our ancestors, and in honor of our descendants, may we choose well. May we choose wisely. May we choose love.

# ACKNOWLEDGMENTS

Many thanks:

To my father, whose memory keeps me always striving to fight the good fight.

To Jonathan Merritt, for getting this book on track for me. At a time when pretty much all I could do was stare at the computer, he came along to save me.

To Thom Hartmann, for explaining so much of the world to me.

To Eleanor LeCain, for expert help and education.

To Ellis Levine, for consistent wisdom and good counsel.

To Mickey Maudlin, for putting up with me and encouraging me at the same time. A fiercely wonderful editor. Also, to Anna Paustenbach, Lisa Zuniga, Laina Adler, Courtney Nobile, Jenn Jensen, and Yvonne Chan at HarperOne.

To my daughter India, for being the most fabulous child a mother could ever hope for.

To Matthew Albracht, Steve Woods, and my brother Peter

Williamson, all of whom added to my understanding of the issues discussed in this book.

To Wendy Zahler, Gina DeVee, Laurie DiBenidetto, Frances Fisher, David Kessler, Victoria Pearman, Alana Stewart, Tammy Vogsland, Paulette Cole, Kirsten Powers, Bruce Bierman, and Bill Seward for the many kindnesses shown.

As always, to the many friends both old and new whom I have met along the way. To readers and audience members . . . friends and teachers all. No words can adequately express my gratitude and love. You have given me such a beautiful life.